Verbal Reasoning

Assessment Papers

Up to Speed

9–10 years

Great Clarendon Street, Oxford, OX2 6DP, United Kingdom

Oxford University Press is a department of the University of Oxford.
It furthers the University's objective of excellence in research,
scholarship, and education by publishing worldwide. Oxford is
a registered trade mark of Oxford University Press in the UK and in
certain other countries

Text © Frances Down 2015

The moral rights of the authors have been asserted

First published in 2015
This edition published in 2022

All rights reserved. No part of this publication may be reproduced,
stored in a retrieval system, or transmitted, in any form or by any
means, without the prior permission in writing of Oxford University
Press, or as expressly permitted by law, by licence or under terms
agreed with the appropriate reprographics rights organization.
Enquiries concerning reproduction outside the scope of the above
should be sent to the Rights Department, Oxford University Press, at
the address above.

You must not circulate this work in any other form and you must
impose this same condition on any acquirer

British Library Cataloguing in Publication Data
Data available

978-0-19-278517-6

10 9 8 7 6 5 4 3

Paper used in the production of this book is a natural, recyclable
product made from wood grown in sustainable forests.
The manufacturing process conforms to the environmental
regulations of the country of origin.

Printed in Great Britain by Ashford Colour Ltd.

Acknowledgements

The publishers would like to thank the following for permissions to
use copyright material:

Page make-up: OKS Prepress, India
Cover illustrations: Lo Cole

Although we have made every effort to trace and contact all
copyright holders before publication this has not been possible in all
cases. If notified, the publisher will rectify any errors or omissions at
the earliest opportunity.

Links to third party websites are provided by Oxford in good faith
and for information only. Oxford disclaims any responsibility for
the materials contained in any third party website referenced in
this work.

The manufacturer's authorised representative in the EU for product safety is
Oxford University Press España S.A. of El Parque Empresarial San Fernando de
Henares, Avenida de Castilla, 2 – 28830 Madrid (www.oup.es/en or product.
safety@oup.com). OUP España S.A. also acts as importer into Spain of
products made by the manufacturer.

Introduction

What is Bond?

The Bond *Up to Speed* titles are part of the Bond range of assessment papers, the number one series for the 11+, selective exams and general practice. Bond *Up to Speed* is carefully designed to support children who need less challenging activities than those in the regular age-appropriate Bond papers, in order to build up and improve their techniques and confidence.

How does this book work?

The book contains two distinct sets of papers, along with full answers and a Progress Chart.

- Focus tests, accompanied by advice and directions, are focused on particular (and age-appropriate) verbal reasoning question types encountered in the 11+ and other exams. The questions are deliberately set at a less challenging level than the standard *Assessment Papers*. Each Focus test is designed to help a child 'catch' their level in a particular question type, and then gently raise it through the course of the test and the subsequent Mixed papers.

- Mixed papers are longer tests containing a full range of verbal reasoning question types. These are designed to provide rigorous practice with less challenging questions, perhaps against the clock, in order to help children acquire and develop the necessary skills and techniques for 11+ success.

Full answers are provided for both types of test in the middle of the book.

How much time should the tests take?

The tests are for practice and to reinforce learning, and you may wish to test exam techniques and working to a set time limit. Using the Mixed papers, we would recommend that your child spends 45 minutes answering the 60 questions in each paper.

You can reduce the suggested time by 5 minutes to practise working at speed.

Using the Progress Chart

The Progress Chart can be used to track Focus test and Mixed paper results over time to monitor how well your child is doing and identify any repeated problems in tackling the different question types.

Focus test 1 — Words that are similar

> Always read this type of question carefully, as most will have similar <u>and</u> opposite options.

Underline the two words in each line that are most similar in type or meaning.

Example   <u>dear</u>   pleasant   poor   extravagant   <u>expensive</u>

> Take care with words, like 'dear', that have more than one meaning. Also watch out for similarly spelled words.

1 right   left   wrong   correct   delay
2 kind   cruel   sort   brave   dirty
3 shut   shout   short   brief   beef
4 spear   sword   dagger   axe   knife
5 pull   push   hall   drag   call
6 year   couple   month   wife   pair

Find a word that is similar in meaning to the word in capital letters and that rhymes with the second word.

Example   CABLE   tyre   <u>WIRE</u>

> Look at the word in capitals. Try to find a suitable similar word. Then experiment with rhyming words.

7 BREEZE   tinned   _____
8 STRIKE   sit   _____
9 COMPLAIN   grown   _____
10 DASH   curry   _____
11 EXPENSE   lost   _____
12 LIFT   days   _____

Underline the two words, one from each group, that are the closest in meaning.

Example   (race, shop, <u>start</u>)   (finish, <u>begin</u>, end)

> Take one word from the left brackets and match it against the words in the right brackets. Repeat until you find a pair that are similar in meaning.

13 (hard, simple, close)   (extra, more, easy)
14 (sweep, creep, weep)   (cry, laugh, run)
15 (lots, less, none)   (few, many, complete)
16 (stay, visit, pile)   (house, ignore, heap)
17 (stick, branch, fruit)   (tree, adhere, eat)
18 (mount, extend, attempt)   (try, chance, opportunity)

Underline the pair of words most similar in meaning.

Example come, go   <u>roams, wanders</u>   fear, fare

19 hide, seek   look, search   calm, busy
20 hilly, flat   black, blue   hint, clue
21 entrance, exit   hare, hair   fury, rage
22 calm, rough   fussy, particular stamp, tiptoe
23 ignorant, knowing suppose, support alter, change
24 stack, pile   store, stone   preserve, claim

> Look for the *most* similar pair.

Underline the word in the brackets that is closest in meaning to the word in capitals.

Example UNHAPPY   (unkind   death   laughter   <u>sad</u>   friendly)

25 QUICK   (slow   fast   safe   needy   blue)
26 STEAL   (roll   roam   rock   robe   rob)
27 SUPERB   (ghastly   ghostly   grisly   excellent entire)
28 BLAST   (nuisance energy   call   hole   explosion)
29 REQUIRE (need   poverty   relapse   relax   select)
30 RULE   (pencil   straight lever   govern   obey)

Now go to the Progress Chart to record your score!   Total   30

Focus test 2 — Words that are opposite

Find a word that is opposite in meaning to the word in capital letters and that rhymes with the second word.

Example QUICK   grow   <u>SLOW</u>

Look at the word in capitals. Try to find a suitable 'opposite' word. Then experiment with rhyming words.

1 COMMON   bear   _____
2 WORK   vest   _____
3 THIN   brick _____
4 FALSE   new   _____
5 UP   noun   _____
6 WIN   news   _____

Underline the two words that are the odd ones out in the following group of words.

Example black   <u>king</u>   purple   green   <u>house</u>

Three of the words have something in common. Look for the link. In the example, it is colours.

7   eye   ear   trousers   glass   nose
8   run   whisper   skip   jump   think
9   apple   cabbage   banana   orange   carrot
10 even   flat   odd   house   bungalow
11 chicken goose   gerbil   rat   duck
12 sixteen three   seven   nine   fourteen

Underline the two words, one from each group, that are the most opposite in meaning.

Example (dawn, <u>early</u>, wake) (<u>late</u>, stop, sunrise)

13 (welcome, left, go) (beside, come, keep)
14 (less, alone, together) (more, some, one)
15 (July, month, winter) (day, autumn, summer)
16 (dry, mild, hot) (humid, cloudy, wet)
17 (cake, slack, educate) (taut, taught, torte)
18 (dark, lamp, moon) (shade, night, light)

Take one word from the left brackets and match it against the words in the right brackets. Repeat until you find a pair of opposites.

Underline the pair of words most opposite in meaning.

Example cup, mug   coffee, milk   <u>hot, cold</u>

19 lie, fib   frog, toad   front, back
20 fire, burn   hill, valley   fruit, vegetable
21 pretty, ugly   finger, thumb   gold, silver
22 hit, miss   stretch, extend   bring, buy
23 aged, old   lift, elevate   start, finish
24 exhaust, tire   expand, contract   climb, ascend

Look for the most opposite pair.

Underline the word in the brackets that is most opposite in meaning to the word in capitals.

Example WIDE (broad   vague   long   <u>narrow</u>   motorway)

25 FULL (complete   heavy   eaten   hungry   empty)
26 APPEAR (vanish   see   seem   vanquish   send)
27 PROFIT (money   loss   lose   loose   gain)
28 BREAK (gap   meant   mend   sorry   sad)
29 LIGHTEN (brighten   darken   fiery   flown   tighten)
30 DANGER (warning   reckless   risky   peril   safety)

Now go to the Progress Chart to record your score!   Total 30

Focus test 3 — Sorting words

Look at these groups of words.

A	B	C
Shapes	Royal titles	Clothes

Choose the correct group for each of the words below. Write in the letter.

1. shirt ____   princess ____
2. king ____   queen ____
3. triangle ____   socks ____
4. sweatshirt ____   square ____
5. prince ____   rectangle ____

Find and underline the two words that need to change places for each sentence to make sense.

Example She went to <u>letter</u> the <u>write</u>.

> Read the sentence carefully and identify where it doesn't make sense.

6. The afternoon fell steadily all rain.
7. He ate his fork with a sausage.
8. The current was easily but the fish swam strong upstream.
9. It was a lovely day sunny.
10. The waves dragging onto the beach crashed the raft ashore.

Rearrange the muddled words in capital letters so that each sentence makes sense.

Example There are sixty SNODCES <u>seconds</u> in a UTMINE <u>minute</u>.

> Use the sense of the sentence to help you. Be careful with spelling.

11. The FRATFCI _____ lights changed to REGNE _____.
12. Look SIDINE _____ our new tent in the DNEGRA _____.
13. I draw straight NESLI _____ with my RRELU _____.
14. Our TIKENT _____ has grown into a big BYATB _____ cat.
15. There are no PETMY _____ TEASS _____ on the bus.

Fill in the crosswords so that all the given words are included. You have been given one letter as a clue in each crossword.

> Use the given letter to place the first word. Then place the other words one by one.

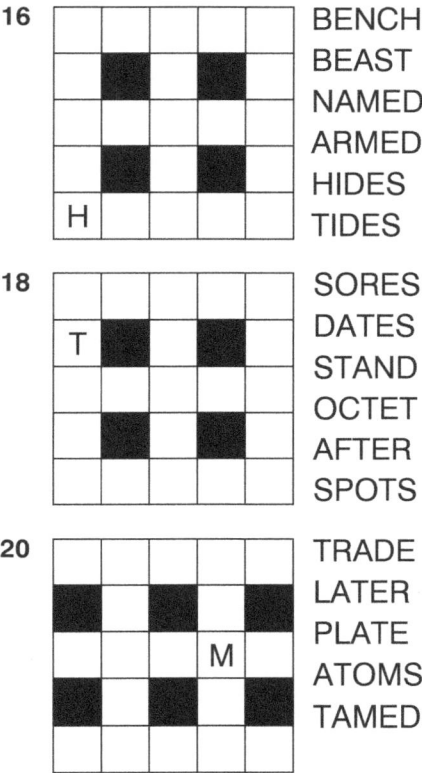

16 BENCH / BEAST / NAMED / ARMED / HIDES / TIDES

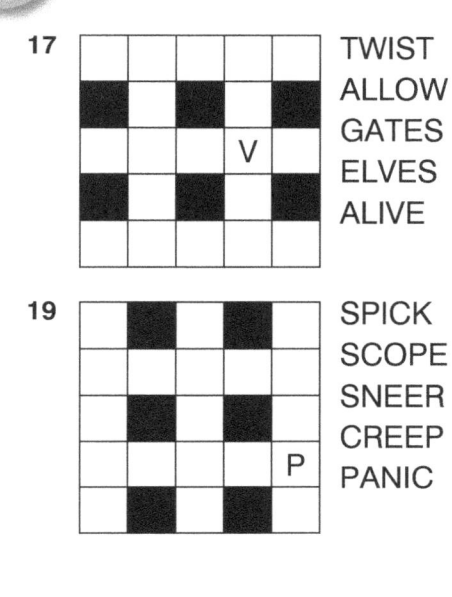

17 TWIST / ALLOW / GATES / ELVES / ALIVE

18 SORES / DATES / STAND / OCTET / AFTER / SPOTS

19 SPICK / SCOPE / SNEER / CREEP / PANIC

20 TRADE / LATER / PLATE / ATOMS / TAMED

Underline the two words in each line that are made from the same letters.

Example   TAP   PET   <u>TEA</u>   POT   <u>EAT</u>

> Scan the words quickly and see if a pair jumps out. If you don't see the answer, look through, word by word, at individual letters.

21	LAID	RAID	RULE	LURE	DARE
22	BALE	DEAL	DALE	BLED	BALL
23	SHOW	WASH	POSH	SHIP	SHOP
24	PART	TART	WART	PORT	TRAP
25	MEAT	MOTE	MOAT	MUTE	ATOM

Rearrange the letters in capitals to make another word. The new word has something to do with the first two words or phrases.

Example spot   soil   SAINT   STAIN

First look at the clues. Then rearrange the letters to find the anagram.

26 jump   spring   PALE   _____
27 glass   sheet   NAPE   _____
28 throb   sore   EACH   _____
29 light   lantern PALM   _____
30 bitter sharp   OURS   _____

Focus test 4 — Selecting words

Complete the following sentences by selecting the most sensible word from each group of words given in the brackets. Underline the words selected.

Example The (<u>children</u>, boxes, foxes) carried the (houses, <u>books</u>, steps) home from the (greengrocer, <u>library</u>, factory).

> Work through the sentence, bracket by bracket, choosing the most appropriate word from each one.

1 If white (balloons, paint, snails) is added to (red, yellow, blue) paint, then you can make a shade of (pink, black, green) paint.

2 When I wake (down, up, on), I open my bedroom (door, carpet, curtains) and look out of my (leg, ceiling, window).

3 If (today, Monday, May) is Saturday, then tomorrow is (Wednesday, Thursday, Sunday) and yesterday was (Thursday, Friday, Saturday).

4 My brother is (baking, cutting, sewing) some (strings, cakes, weeds) and the smell is (dusty, untidy, delicious).

5 Polar (bears, moles, cats) live in the (jungle, Arctic, cupboard) and hunt seals for (drink, fun, food).

Choose the word or phrase that makes each sentence true.

Example A LIBRARY always has (posters, a carpet, <u>books</u>, DVDs, stairs).

> Think about what the word in capitals <u>has</u> to have.

6 A LAKE always has (waves, boats, water, fish, islands).

7 A JUNGLE always has (monkeys, plants, elephants, waterfalls, roads).

8 A PAIR OF BOOTS always has (laces, mud, an owner, soles, holes).

9 A COW always has (horns, milk, grass, hooves, calves).

10 A BOX always has (sides, a flap, a lining, a surprise, chocolates).

Underline the one word in brackets that will go equally well with both the pairs of words outside the brackets.

Example   rush, attack   cost, fee   (price, hasten, strike, <u>charge</u>, money)

> The answer might have two very different meanings. Check your answer goes with <u>both</u> pairs of words.

11   caring, generous   type, sort   (considerate, kind, nature, nurse, arrange)

12   extremity, end   empty out, pour   (overbalance, fall, tip, nib, edge)

13   attach, fasten   dead heat, same level   (tie, connect, link, equal, bolt)

14   knock, rap   controls water, a pipe stop   (hot, cold, tap, strike, blow)

15   pen, yard   hit, beat   (batter, hammer, money, crush, pound)

Underline two words, one from each group, that go together to form a new word. The word in the first group always comes first.

Example   (hand, <u>green</u>, for)   (light, <u>house</u>, sure)

> Take one word at a time from the left brackets and put it in front of each of the words in the right brackets.

16   (star, swim, car)   (pet, pull, pit)

17   (sauce, pot, spilt)   (twin, flour, pan)

18   (pea, bean, swede)   (net, nut, not)

19   (tire, car, wheel)   (some, there, few)

20   (rot, make, best)   (ten, nine, four)

Underline the one word in each group that **cannot be made** from the letters of the word in capital letters.

Example STATIONERY   stone   tyres   ration   <u>nation</u>   noisy

> Look for any letters that are not in the word in capitals and for repeats of letters.

21	BRAMBLE	lamb	barb	real	pram	male
22	COTTAGE	gate	sage	goat	teat	cage
23	PICTURE	pure	tire	epic	care	true
24	SPATULA	trap	laps	past	last	pals
25	KINGDOM	monk	mink	dong	mind	dine

Underline the one word in each group that **can be made** from the letters of the word in capital letters.

Example CHAMPION   camping   notch   peach   cramp   <u>chimp</u>

> This time, only one word can be made from the word in capitals. Look, particularly, at the vowels.

26	LETTUCE	cute	teal	feet	tuck	cell
27	EXCITED	site	dent	toxic	text	dice
28	JUGGLED	deal	lead	glad	jade	glue
29	PHANTOM	chat	moat	tone	then	shop
30	DAZZLED	jazz	sled	eddy	read	zeal

Focus test 5 — Selecting letters

Which one letter can be added to the front of all of these words to make new words?

Example   __are   __at   __rate   __all   <u>c</u>

> Experiment with putting various letters in front of each of the words until you find the correct one.

1 __lasted   __read   __link   __lender   __
2 __ending   __ode   __ate   __allow   __
3 __lope   __very   __merge   __at   __
4 __trapping   __tart   __welling   __witch   __
5 __our   __east   __ourselves   __ear   __

Find the letter that will end the first word and start the second word.

Example   drow (<u>n</u>) ought

6 crea (__) onkey
7 polic (__) ndless
8 part (__) oung
9 nigh (__) witch
10 spel (__) augh

> Look at the word on the left and find various letters that could finish that word. Then see which one you can also use to start the word on the right.

Find the letter that will complete both pairs of words, ending the first word and starting the second. The same letter must be used for both pairs of words.

Example   mea (<u>t</u>) able   fi (<u>t</u>) ub

11 walkin (__) reen   flun (__) lide
12 kick (__) wallow   bat (__) alt
13 niec (__) lder   budg (__) very
14 himsel (__) inger   hoo (__) aster
15 pa (__) illow   co (__) indow

Move one letter from the first word to the second word to make two new words.

Example hunt   sip   <u>hut</u>   <u>snip</u>

> Take a letter at a time from the first word and see if you can make a separate word. Then see if you can put the letter into the second word to make a new word.

16 pipe   hum   _____   _____
17 pant   hit   _____   _____
18 clap   art   _____   _____
19 bite   not   _____   _____
20 home   end   _____   _____

Add one letter to the word in capital letters to make a new word. The meaning of the new word is given in the clue.

> Add suitable letters to the word in capitals and think about the meaning to help you. Alternatively, you could look at the meaning and find a word that uses the letters given on the left.

Example PLAN   simple   <u>PLAIN</u>

21 BOTH   soup   _____
22 NICE   relation   _____
23 PACE   calm   _____
24 LUCK   fortunate   _____
25 SAME   disgrace   _____

Remove one letter from the word in capital letters to leave a new word. The meaning of the new word is given in the clue.

Example AUNT   an insect   <u>ANT</u>

26 CLAPS   hats   _____
27 SIGHT   breathe out   _____
28 STEAM   stalk   _____
29 BEAST   finest   _____
30 FLAIR   den   _____

Now go to the Progress Chart to record your score!   Total   30

Focus test 6 — Finding words

Change one word so that the sentence makes sense. Underline the word you are taking out and write your new word on the line.

Example I waited in line to buy a <u>book</u> to see the film.   ticket

1 Giraffes have short necks to reach leaves in high trees. _____

2 My ice pebble dribbled down the cone. _____

3 George blew the presents out on his birthday cake as we sang 'Happy Birthday'. _____

4 The sun shone and clouds blew across the green sky. _____

Find the three-letter word that can be added to the letters in capitals to make a new word. The new word will complete the sentence sensibly. Write the three-letter word.

Example The cat sprang onto the MO.   USE

5 I carried the supermarket BET for my mother. _____

6 Archie has entered the school singing COMITION. _____

7 We watched the RHORSES gallop fast up the racetrack. _____

8 She knew they loved fruit, so she brought a bag of CRIES with her. _____

9 On URDAY, we are going to have a barbecue _____

Find a word that can be put in front of each of the following words to make new, compound words.

Example cast   fall   ward   pour   <u>down</u>

> Look for common words such as up/down, hand/foot, and so on.

10 stage	shore	ward	line	_____
11 fly	cup	nut	fingers	_____
12 gammon	ground	pack	bone	_____
13 shine	light	day	bathe	_____

Change the first word of the third pair in the same way as the other pairs to give a new word.

Example bind, hind   bare, hare   but, <u>hut</u>

See how the letters have been changed and continue the pattern. Take care with letter order.

14 feel, eel   claw, law   pray, _____
15 nut, net   but, bet   gut, _____
16 fan, wan   fool, wool   find, _____
17 damp, dam   herd, her   then, _____

Write the four-letter word hidden at the end of one word and the beginning of the next word in each sentence. The order of the letters may not be changed.

Example We had bat<u>s and</u> balls.   <u>sand</u>

Work carefully through the sentence, word by word. Sound out the possibilities.

18 The sugary water trap caught loads of insects.   _____
19 Please attend carefully to what I am saying.   _____
20 Snow fell overnight and covered the street.   _____
21 My computer makes a funny noise starting up.   _____
22 The road home was blocked by an overturned bus. _____

Look at the first group of three words. The word in the middle has been made from the two other words. Complete the second group of three words in the same way, making a new word in the middle of the group.

Example PAIN   INT<u>O</u>   TO<u>OK</u>   ALSO   <u>SOON</u>   ONLY

Letter by letter, see where the middle word gets its letters from. Repeat the pattern for the second group of words.

23 CALM   CART   FORT   HUNG   _____   LIMP
24 POOL   PEEL   MEET   BARK   _____   FOOL
25 JEST   JAMS   RAMS   BILL   _____   DONE
26 MESH   RUSH   TRUE   PICK   _____   CLUE

Change the first word into the last word by changing one letter at a time and making a new, different word in the middle.

Example CASE <u>CASH</u> LASH

> Write down the letters that remain the same. Substitute the remaining letters one at a time.

27 COOL _____ HOOK
28 MADE _____ TALE
29 FORK _____ FOND
30 BEAT _____ COAT

Focus test 7 — Logic

Read the first two statements and then underline the one option that must be true.

> Look for the statement that <u>has</u> to be true, using only the information you have been given.

1. Letters contain information. Letters are put into envelopes before posting.
   - A Envelopes may have important letters in them.
   - B Our postal service is good.
   - C Birthday cards come in the post.
   - D All letters have white envelopes.

2. All dogs should have collars. Some collars are made of leather.
   - A All dogs have red collars.
   - B A dog I know has a cloth collar.
   - C A cat could have a collar.
   - D A dog could have a leather collar.

3. A square has four equal sides. Squares are a type of shape.
   - A All shapes have four equal sides.
   - B A rectangle is like a square.
   - C Some shapes have four sides.
   - D A triangle has three sides.

Four friends, 1, 2, 3 and 4, like different foods. Friends 1 and 2 like pasta. The other two prefer rice. Friends 1 and 4 like sausages and chips. Friends 2 and 3 prefer curry. All of them like chicken except 1.

> Before you answer the questions, write down the foods and which child likes what.

4. Which is the most popular food? _____
5. Who likes pasta as well as chicken? _____
6. Who likes curry and rice, but not sausages and chips? _____

Eli's house is opposite mine. Mine is number 27. I live on the odd side of the road, he lives on the even side. There are forty houses altogether. If number 1 is opposite number 2 and 3 is opposite 4 and so on, answer these questions.

> Before you start, work out the pattern on a piece of paper.

7 Which house is opposite number 8? ____

8 What is Eli's house number? ____

9 One of Eli's next-door neighbours lives at number 26. What number is his other next-door neighbour? ____

10 One of my next-door neighbours lives at number 25. What number is my other next-door neighbour? ____

11 Asif lives in the house opposite number 37. What number house does he live in? ____

Ananya has six felt pens that she keeps in a case. Below is a diagram of it. From the information, work out the order in which she keeps her pens.

1	2	3	4	5	6
			YELLOW		

The blue pen is between, and next to, the red pen and the green pen. The purple pen is not next to the yellow pen, neither is the green pen next to the yellow. The red pen is two places away from the orange pen. In which place number is each of the colour pens?

> Write a list of the pen colours and their possible positions. Eliminate the positions as you read through the information.

12 blue ____   13 red ____   14 green ____
15 purple ____   16 orange ____

Here is a train timetable.

| BILSTON (depart) | 09:00 | 10:00 | 11:00 | 12:00 |
| WAVENEY (arrive) | 09:45 | 10:45 | 11:45 | 12:45 |

17 How long does the journey take from Bilston to Waveney? ____

18 If the 10:00 train arrived 15 minutes late, what time would I arrive at Waveney? ____

19 If I have an appointment in Waveney at midday, which train should I catch from Bilston? ____

Using the map on the right, underline the correct compass points in the questions.

20 Town A is to the (west, north, east) of Town D.

21 Town C is to the (east, west, south) of Town B.

22 To travel from Town C to Town A, you must travel first (west, north, east) and then north.

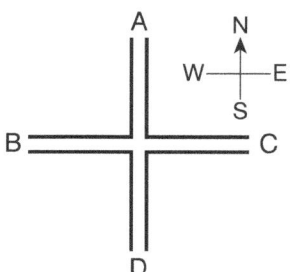

Maya is six years younger than Charlie, who is nine years older than Kyle, who is 8. How old is:

23 Charlie? _____   24 Maya? _____

If yesterday was Monday, answer these questions.

25 Which day of the week was it a week ago from today? _____

26 What is the day after tomorrow? _____

27 What is the day two days ago from today? _____

Jason has £20 more savings than Kirsten, who has £17 less savings than Kieran, who has £34 savings. How much does each person have?

28 Kirsten _____   29 Jason _____

30 If Caitlin was 8 when her cousin, Tina, was born and she is 13 now, how old is Tina? _____

Focus test 8 — Substitution and alphabetical order

If a = 4, b = 5, c = 3 and d = 2, find the value of the following calculations.

1. a + b + c = ____
2. c × b = ____
3. (d + b) − c = ____
4. a ÷ d = ____
5. (c + d) − a = ____
6. 3b − (a ÷ d) = ____

Replace the letters with numbers and work out the calculations.

If b = 1, r = 2, e = 3, a = 4 and d = 5, what are the totals of these words?

7. read ____
8. bear ____
9. babe ____
10. dear ____
11. bead ____
12. deed ____

Add each of the letter values together to make a word total.

If the letters in the following words are arranged in alphabetical order, which letter comes in the middle?

13. CRIME ____
14. BARGE ____
15. DWELT ____
16. MINUS ____
17. SPORT ____
18. FOXED ____

Write the letters of each word in alphabetical order, then pick out the middle one.

> Write the words in alphabetical order before you begin.

    LEMON   APPLE   ORANGE   BANANA   PEACH

If these fruits are put into alphabetical order, which comes:

19 first? _____

20 third? _____

21 last? _____

    SPELL   RAMPS   REALM   POSTS   SNAKE

If these words are put into alphabetical order, which comes:

22 second? _____

23 fourth? _____

24 last? _____

    MERRY   MAGIC   MUMPS   MILKY   MOONS

If these words are put into alphabetical order, which comes:

25 second? _____

26 fourth? _____

27 fifth? _____

If the days of the week are put into alphabetical order, which comes:

28 first? _____

29 after Saturday? _____

30 after Tuesday? _____

Focus test 9 Codes

The code for FLOWER is 9 5 0 3 1 4. Encode each of these words using the same code.

> First line up the code with the word.
> F L O W E R
> 9 5 0 3 1 4
> Then substitute the letters for numbers.

1 FLOW _____
2 WERE _____

Decode these words using the same code as above.

3 9 1 1 5 _____
4 3 0 5 9 _____

The code for FATHER is % ? > < * +. Encode each of these words using the same code.

5 FATE _____
6 AREA _____

Decode these words using the same code as above.

7 > + * * _____
8 < ? > * _____

The code for EATING is h v f s w p. Encode each of these words using the same code.

9 NEAT _____
10 GNAT _____

> Make sure you write the code letters in lower case, not capitals.

Decode these words using the same code as above.

11 p v f h _____
12 p v s w _____

These words have been written in code, but the codes are not written under the right words. Match the right code to each word given below.

SOUP	POOL	LOOP	POUR
Y N D V	X N D Y	Y N N Z	Z N N Y

13 Y N N Z _____

14 X N D Y _____

15 Y N D V _____

16 Z N N Y _____

Look for letters that stand out. Here, two words begin with P and one has a double O.

17 Using the same code, encode PLUS. _____

18 If the code for FABLE is H T O W X, encode FEEL. _____

19 Using the same code as for FABLE, decode O T W X. _____

20 If the code for DIRTY is 7 3 5 1 8, encode TIDY. _____

21 Using the same code as for DIRTY, decode 1 5 8. _____

22 If the code for BRAIN is = + / # !, encode BARN. _____

23 Using the same code as for BRAIN, decode = / + =. _____

24 If the code for CRANE is s p m v z, encode CARE. _____

25 Using the same code as for CRANE, decode v z m p. _____

The code for SPREADING is * Q 2 3 z U 4 > k. Encode each of these words using the same code.

26 SEED _____

27 IDEA _____

Take care with writing the codes correctly.

Decode these words using the same code as above.

28 2 z 4 > _____

29 Q z k 3 _____

30 Q 3 z 2 _____

Focus test 10 Sequences

Complete the following sentences in the best way by choosing one word from each set of brackets.

Example Tall is to (tree, <u>short</u>, colour) as narrow is to (thin, white, <u>wide</u>).

> Find the relationship between the pairs of statements. The second pairing must be completed in the same way as the first pairing.

1. Hard is to (soft, difficult, wood) as wet is to (dry, water, droplet).
2. Fish is to (hook, scales, swim) as bird is to (goose, fly, sky).
3. Reply is to (touch, answer, write) as silly is to (sensible, foolish, responsible).
4. Impossible is to (possible, easy, fair) as impolite is to (rude, polite, quiet).
5. See is to (foot, saw, eye) as hear is to (there, ear, sound).
6. Rich is to (poor, money, strong) as take is to (tack, give, steal).

Fill in the missing letters. The alphabet has been written out to help you.

A B C D E F G H I J K L M N O P Q R S T U V W X Y Z

Example AB is to CD as PQ is to <u>RS</u>.

> Look for the pattern in these sequences. Try putting your finger on the alphabet line and counting the number of spaces.

7. EF is to GH as UV is to ___.
8. TS is to RQ as PO is to ___.
9. DF is to HJ as LN is to ___.
10. OP is to QR as ST is to ___.
11. GG is to HH as II is to ___.
12. IH is to GF as ___ is ED to ___.

Focus test 1: Words that are similar (pages 4–5)

1. **right, correct** 'Right' and 'correct' both mean accurate or exact.
2. **kind, sort** 'Kind' and 'sort' both mean a type of something.
3. **short, brief** 'Short' and 'brief' both mean for a little length of time.
4. **dagger, knife** A 'dagger' is a type of 'knife' or cutting tool.
5. **pull, drag** 'Pull' and 'drag' both mean to tug or haul.
6. **couple, pair** 'Couple' and 'pair' both mean two of something.
7. WIND
8. HIT
9. MOAN
10. HURRY
11. COST
12. RAISE
13. **simple, easy** 'Simple' and 'easy' both mean uncomplicated.
14. **weep, cry** 'Weep' and 'cry' both mean to be tearful, to sob.
15. **lots, many** 'Lots' and 'many' both mean a large number or amount.
16. **pile, heap** 'Pile' and 'heap' both mean a mound of something.
17. **stick, adhere** 'Stick' and 'adhere' both mean to glue two things together.
18. **attempt, try** 'Attempt' and 'try' both mean to have a go at something.
19. **look, search**
20. **hint, clue**
21. **fury, rage**
22. **fussy, particular**
23. **alter, change**
24. **stack, pile**
25. **fast** 'Quick' and 'fast' both mean speedy.
26. **rob** 'Steal' and 'rob' both mean to take something that is not yours.
27. **excellent** 'Superb' and 'excellent' both mean of a very high standard.
28. **explosion** 'Blast' and 'explosion' both mean a bang or burst.
29. **need** 'Require' and 'need' both mean to want something because it is essential or necessary.
30. **govern** 'Rule' and 'govern' both mean to lead and control.

Focus test 2: Words that are opposite (pages 6–7)

1. RARE
2. REST
3. THICK
4. TRUE
5. DOWN
6. LOSE
7. **trousers, glass** The other words are features of the face.
8. **whisper, think** The other words are all physical actions or movements.
9. **cabbage, carrot** The other words are all fruit.
10. **even, odd** The other words are types of housing.
11. **gerbil, rat** The other words are all birds.
12. **sixteen, fourteen** The other words are all single-digit odd numbers.
13. **go, come** 'Go' is to move further away whereas 'come' means to approach nearer.
14. **less, more** 'Less' means fewer whereas 'more' means an increase in number.
15. **winter, summer** 'Winter' is the coldest season whereas 'summer' is the hottest season.
16. **dry, wet** 'Dry' means without water whereas 'wet' is well watered.
17. **slack, taut** 'Slack' means loose whereas 'taut' is pulled tight.
18. **dark, light** 'Dark' is without light like night-time whereas 'light' means you can see as in daytime.
19. **front, back** 'Front' is the part of something that faces outwards and is visible whereas 'back' is the rear or unseen part of something.
20. **hill, valley** A 'hill' is a mound or lump of ground whereas a 'valley' is a dip or depression in the landscape.
21. **pretty, ugly** 'Pretty' is attractive whereas 'ugly' is unattractive.
22. **hit, miss** A 'hit' is successful whereas a 'miss' is unsuccessful.
23. **start, finish** 'Start' is the beginning whereas 'finish' is the end.
24. **expand, contract** 'Expand' means to get bigger whereas 'contract' is to get smaller.
25. **empty** 'Full' means complete or replete whereas 'empty' means there is nothing in it.
26. **vanish** 'Appear' means to become visible whereas 'vanish' means to disappear.
27. **loss** A 'profit' is when you make money, whereas a 'loss' is when you lose money.
28. **mend** To 'break' is to damage something whereas to 'mend' is to repair it.
29. **darken** 'Lighten' means to become brighter, with more light, making it easier to see, whereas 'darken' is to lose light making it harder to see.
30. **safety** 'Danger' means peril whereas 'safety' is a haven.

Focus test 3: Sorting words (pages 8–10)

1–5 Category A contains Shapes (triangle, square, rectangle)
Category B contains Royal titles (princess, king, queen, prince)
Category C contains Clothes (shirt, socks, sweatshirt)

EXPANDED ANSWERS

1 C, B
2 B, B
3 A, C
4 C, A
5 B, A
6 The **rain** fell steadily all **afternoon**.
7 He ate his **sausage** with a **fork**.
8 The current was **strong** but the fish swam **easily** upstream.
9 It was a lovely **sunny day**.
10 The waves **crashed** onto the beach **dragging** the raft ashore.
11 traffic, green
12 inside, garden
13 lines, ruler
14 kitten, tabby
15 empty, seats

16

B	E	A	S	T
E		R		I
N	A	M	E	D
C		E		E
H	I	D	E	S

17

G	A	T	E	S
	L		L	
A	L	I	V	E
	O		E	
T	W	I	S	T

18

S	P	O	T	S
T		C		O
A	F	T	E	R
N		E		E
D	A	T	E	S

19

S		S		S
P	A	N	I	C
I		E		O
C	R	E	E	P
K		R		E

20

P	L	A	T	E
	A		A	
A	T	O	M	S
	E		E	
T	R	A	D	E

21 RULE, LURE
22 DEAL, DALE
23 POSH, SHOP
24 PART, TRAP
25 MOAT, ATOM
26 LEAP
27 PANE
28 ACHE
29 LAMP
30 SOUR

Focus test 4: Selecting words
(pages 11–13)

1–5 Try each of the words in the first set of brackets. Do they make sense with any words in the second and third sets of brackets? Only one combination of three words makes sense.

1 paint, red, pink
2 up, curtains, window
3 today, Sunday, Friday
4 baking, cakes, delicious
5 bears, Arctic, food
6 **water** A lake is made up of water. It may or may not have the other things.
7 **plants** A jungle is made up of plants with animals and water in it too.
8 **soles** A pair of boots has to have soles whereas it may or may not have the other things.
9 **hooves** All cows have hooves as a part of their bodies; only some types of cow have horns.
10 **sides** A box is a shape which must have sides or it would collapse.
11 **kind** 'Kind' can mean generous and caring; it can also mean a type of something.
12 **tip** A 'tip' can mean the extremity or far end of something (e.g. the tip of a pen); it can also mean to pour or empty out something from a container.
13 **tie** To 'tie' can mean to attach or fasten something; a 'tie' means a dead heat in a race or a game.
14 **tap** To 'tap' means to knock or rap; a 'tap' is an appliance that controls the flow of water.
15 **pound** A 'pound' can mean a pen or yard in which things are stored; to 'pound' means to hit something hard and repeatedly.
16 carpet
17 saucepan
18 peanut
19 tiresome
20 rotten
21 **pram** There is no 'P' in BRAMBLE.
22 **sage** There is no 'S' in COTTAGE.
23 **care** There is no 'A' in PICTURE.

A2

24 **trap** There is no 'R' in SPATULA.
25 **dine** There is no 'E' in KINGDOM.
26 **cute**
27 **dice**
28 **glue**
29 **moat**
30 **zeal**

Focus test 5: Selecting letters
(pages 14–15)

1 **b** blasted, bread, blink, blender
2 **m** mending, mode, mate, mallow
3 **e** elope, every, emerge, eat
4 **s** strapping, start, swelling, switch
5 **y** your, yeast, yourselves, year
6 **m** cream, monkey
7 **e** police, endless
8 **y** party, young
9 **t** night, twitch
10 **l** spell, laugh
11 **g** walking, green; flung, glide
12 **s** kicks, swallow; bats, salt
13 **e** niece, elder; budge, every
14 **f** himself, finger; hoof, faster
15 **w** paw, willow; cow, window
16 **p** pie, hump
17 **n** pat, hint
18 **c** lap, cart
19 **e** bit, note
20 **m** hoe, mend
21 **BR**OTH
22 **NI**E**CE**
23 **P**E**ACE**
24 **LUCK**Y
25 **SH**AME
26 **CAPS**
27 **SIGH**
28 **STEM**
29 **BEST**
30 **LAIR**

Focus test 6: Finding words
(pages 16–18)

1 **short, long** Giraffes have long necks to reach leaves in high trees.
2 **pebble, cream** My ice cream dribbled down the cone.
3 **presents, candles** George blew the candles out on his birthday cake as we sang 'Happy Birthday'.
4 **green, blue** The sun shone and the clouds blew across the blue sky.
5 **ASK** basket
6 **PET** competition

7 **ACE** racehorses
8 **HER** cherries
9 **SAT** Saturday
10 **on** onstage, onshore, onward, online
11 **butter** butterfly, buttercup, butternut, butterfingers
12 **back** backgammon, background, backpack, backbone
13 **sun** sunshine, sunlight, Sunday, sunbathe
14 **ray** The pattern is to remove the first letter of the first word.
15 **get** The pattern is to remove the middle letter in the first word, 'u', and replace it with 'e'.
16 **wind** The pattern is to remove 'f' from the beginning of the first word and replace it with 'w'.
17 **the** The pattern is to remove the last letter of the first word.
18 **fins** The sugary water trap caught loads o**f ins**ects.
19 **seat** Plea**se at**tend carefully to what I am saying.
20 **love** Snow fel**l ove**rnight and covered the street.
21 **term** My compu**ter m**akes a funny noise starting up.
22 **hero** T**he ro**ad home was blocked by an overturned bus.
23 **HUMP**

1	2				3	4
C	A	L	M		F	O	R	T

1	2				3	4
H	U	N	G		L	I	M	P

24 **BOOK**

1			4		2/3*	2/3*	
P	O	O	L		M	E	E	T

1			4		2/3*	2/3*	
B	A	R	K		F	O	O	L

25 **BONE**

1		4*			2	3	4*
J	E	S	T		R	A	M	S

1		4*			2	3	4*
B	I	L	L		D	O	N	E

26 **LUCK**

		3	4		1	2	
M	E	S	H		T	R	U	E

		3	4		1	2	
P	I	C	K		C	L	U	E

27 COOK
28 MALE
29 FORD
30 BOAT

Focus test 7: Logic (pages 19–21)

1 **A Envelopes may have important letters in them.** B, C and D may be true but A is the correct answer because letters could be important and they are posted in envelopes.
2 **D A dog could have a leather collar.** A is not true as collars come in all colours. B and C may be true. D is the correct answer as a collar could be leather.
3 **C Some shapes have four sides.** Here, you must use the given information which mentions squares have four sides and are a type of shape. Therefore, the answer is C. A is incorrect and B and D are not referred to in the information.
4–6 Use a grid to help you:

	Pasta	Rice	Sausages and chips	Curry	Chicken
1	✓		✓		
2	✓			✓	✓
3		✓		✓	✓
4		✓	✓		✓

4 **chicken**
5 **2**
6 **3**
7–11 Use a chart to help you:

1	3	5	7	9	11	13	15	17	19	21	23	25	27	29	31	33	35	37	39
-	-	-	-	-	-	-	S	T	R	E	E	T	-	-	-	-	-	-	-
2	4	6	8	10	12	14	16	18	20	22	24	26	28	30	32	34	36	38	40

7 **7**
8 **28**
9 **30**
10 **29**
11 **38**
12–16 From the information you know that red and green are next to and either side of blue, therefore blue has to be 2. Green cannot be next to yellow, so is 1, leaving red in 3. Orange is two places away from red (3) so is in 5, leaving purple in 6 not next to the yellow.
12 **2**
13 **3**
14 **1**
15 **6**
16 **5**
17 **45 minutes** 09:00 to 09:45 is 45 minutes' journey time.
18 **11:00** The train should arrive at 10:45. If it was 15 minutes late, it would arrive at 11:00.
19 **11:00** The 11:00 train will arrive in Waveney at 11:45 which is before 12:00.
20 **north** Town A is directly above Town D, so it is to the north.
21 **east** Town C is to the right of Town B, so it is to the east.
22 **west** From Town C, you must first go to the left or west, to reach the centre and then northwards to Town A.
23–24 You know Kyle is 8. Charlie is 9 years older so he is 17 (8 + 9). Maya is 6 years younger than Charlie so 11 (17 – 6).
23 **17**
24 **11**
25–27 Use a chart to help you:

Yesterday	Monday
Today	Tuesday
Tomorrow	Wednesday
Day after tomorrow	Thursday

25 **Tuesday** If it is Tuesday today, a week ago from today it was also Tuesday.
26 **Thursday** Tuesday is today, tomorrow is Wednesday and the day after tomorrow is Thursday.
27 **Sunday** If today is Tuesday, yesterday was Monday and the day before that was Sunday.
28–30 You know that Kieran has £34. Kirsten has £17 less than Kieran so has £17 (34 – 17 = 17). Jason has £20 more than Kirsten so has £37 (17 + 20 = 37).
28 **£17**
29 **£37**
30 **5** 13 – 8 = 5

Focus test 8: Substitution and alphabetical order (pages 22–23)

1 **12** 4 + 5 + 3 = 12
2 **15** 3 × 5 = 15
3 **4** (2 + 5) – 3 = 4
4 **2** 4 ÷ 2 = 2
5 **1** (3 + 2) – 4 = 1
6 **13** (3 × 5) – (4 ÷ 2) = 15 – 2 = 13
7 **14** 2 + 3 + 4 + 5 = 14
8 **10** 1 + 3 + 4 + 2 = 10
9 **9** 1 + 4 + 1 + 3 = 9
10 **14** 5 + 3 + 4 + 2 = 14
11 **13** 1 + 3 + 4 + 5 = 13
12 **16** 5 + 3 + 3 + 5 = 16
13 **I** CRIME = CEIMR
14 **E** BARGE = ABEGR
15 **L** DWELT = DELTW
16 **N** MINUS = IMNSU
17 **R** SPORT = OPRST
18 **F** FOXED = DEFOX

19–21 Use a grid to help you:

L	E	M	O	N		3
A	P	P	L	E		1
O	R	A	N	G	E	4
B	A	N	A	N	A	2
P	E	A	C	H		5

19 **APPLE**
20 **LEMON**
21 **PEACH**

22–24 Use a grid to help you:

S	P	E	L	L	5
R	A	M	P	S	2
R	E	A	L	M	3
P	O	S	T	S	1
S	N	A	K	E	4

22 **RAMPS**
23 **SNAKE**
24 **SPELL**

25–27 Use a grid to help you:

M	E	R	R	Y	2
M	A	G	I	C	1
M	U	M	P	S	5
M	I	L	K	Y	3
M	O	O	N	S	4

25 **MERRY**
26 **MOONS**
27 **MUMPS**

28–30 Put the days of the week into alphabetical order first:

F	R	I	D	A	Y			1
M	O	N	D	A	Y			2
S	A	T	U	R	D	A	Y	3
S	U	N	D	A	Y			4
T	H	U	R	S	D	A	Y	5
T	U	E	S	D	A	Y		6
W	E	D	N	E	S	D	A	Y	7

28 **Friday**
29 **Sunday**
30 **Wednesday**

Focus test 9: Codes (pages 24–25)

1 **9503** F = 9, L = 5, O = 0, W = 3
2 **3141** W = 3, E = 1, R = 4, E = 1
3 **FEEL** 9 = F, 1 = E, 1 = E, 5 = L
4 **WOLF** 3 = W, 0 = O, 5 = L, 9 = F
5 **% ? > *** F = %, A = ?, T = >, E = *
6 **? + * ?** A = ?, R = +, E = *, A = ?
7 **TREE** > = T, + = R, * = E, * = E
8 **HATE** < = H, ? = A, > = T, * = E
9 **w h v f** N = w, E = h, A = v, T = f
10 **p w v f** G = p, N = w, A = v, T = f
11 **GATE** p = G, v = A, f = T, h = E
12 **GAIN** p = G, v = A, s = I, w = N
13–17 Two of the words begin with 'P' so P = Y. 'POOL', because it begins with 'Y' and has a double letter in the middle must be YNNZ. Therefore POUR = YNDV and LOOP = ZNNY as it, too, has a double letter, leaving SOUP = XNDY.

13 **POOL**
14 **SOUP**
15 **POUR**
16 **LOOP**
17 **YZDX** Y = P, Z = L, U = D, S = X
18 **HXXW** F = H, E = X, E = X, L = W
19 **BALE** O = B, T = A, W = L, X = E
20 **1378** T = 1, I = 3, D = 7, Y = 8
21 **TRY** 1 = T, 5 = R, 8 = Y
22 **= / + !** B = =, A = /, R = +, N = !
23 **BARB** = = B, / = A, + = R, = = B
24 **s m p z** C = s, A = m, R = p, E = z
25 **NEAR** v = N, z = E, m = A, p = R
26 *** 3 3 U** * = S, 3 = E, 3 = E, D = U
27 **4 U 3 z** I = 4, D = U, E = 3, A = z
28 **RAIN** 2 = R, z = A, 4 = I, > = N
29 **PAGE** Q = P, z = A, k = G, 3 = E
30 **PEAR** Q = P, 3 = E, z = A, 2 = R

Focus test 10: Sequences (pages 26–27)

1 **soft, dry** 'Hard' is the opposite of 'soft' in the same way as 'wet' is opposite to 'dry'.
2 **swim, fly** A 'fish' 'swims' in the same way a 'bird' 'flies'.
3 **answer, foolish** 'Reply' is similar to 'answer' in the same way as 'silly' is similar to 'foolish'.
4 **possible, polite** 'Impossible' is the opposite of 'possible' in the same way as 'impolite' is opposite to 'polite'.
5 **eye, ear** You 'see' with your 'eye' as you 'hear' with your 'ear'.
6 **poor, give** 'Rich' is the opposite of 'poor' in the same way as 'take' is the opposite of 'give'.
7 **WX** Each letter in the first pair moves forwards two places.
8 **NM** Each letter in the first pair moves backwards two places.
9 **PR** Each letter in the first pair moves forwards four places.
10 **UV** Each letter in the first pair moves forwards two places.

11	**JJ** This is a repeating pattern with each pair of letters moving forwards one place, so II becomes JJ.	1	**circus, tickets, evening**
		2	**kittens, weeks, playing**
		3	**supermarkets, fuel, food**
12	**CB** Each letter in the first pair moves backwards two places.	4	**noise, roadworks, ache**
		5	**birthday, cards, parcels**
13–19	There are two ways of working out these answers. The first approach (Q13–16) looks at all the letters in each question as a continuous sequence. The second approach (Q17–19) looks at each letter in a pair individually.	6	**APE** paper
		7	**ATE** later
		8	**TEN** kittens
		9	**LIP** slippery
		10	**OWE** lawnmower
13	**IJ, KL** Each pair is the next two letters in the alphabet.	11	**s** soften, sink, sinner, selfish
		12	**h** herring, hanger, hours, hate
14	**RS, UV** After each pair, skip one letter in the alphabet then write the next two, e.g. FG (H) IJ (K) LM (N) OP (Q) RS (T) UV.	13	**b** border, blasting, brainy, blame
		14	**f** flash, falter, flung, fright
		15	**v** van, vomit, valley, vague
15	**QS, UW** These are the alternate letters of the alphabet starting with A, arranged in pairs.	16	**28** 11 + 17 = 28
		17	**34** 5 + 9 + 20 = 34
16	**JH, FD** These are alternate letters of the alphabet in reverse order starting with Z, arranged in pairs.	18	**44** 14 + 17 + 13 = 44
		19	**December** 20 + 9 = 29
		20	**Stefan's** Stefan supports the blue team. RED = 5 + 9 + 20 + 12 + 11 + 13 = 70; BLUE = 7 + 11 + 9 + 14 + 17 + 13 = 71
17	**DE, GF** The first letters in each pair are in a repeating pattern: DGDGDG. The second letters move forwards one place.		
18	**YJ, ZK** Each letter in each pair moves forward one place.	21–25	Category A Languages: French, Greek, Spanish Category B Colours: yellow, red, purple, black Category C Trees: beech, cherry, oak
19	**VN, UL** The first letter in each pair moves backwards one place. The second letter moves backwards two places.	21	**A, B**
		22	**C, B**
		23	**B, B**
20	**CN, AJ** The first letter in each pair moves backwards two places. The second letters are in a repeating pattern: NJNJNJ.	24	**C, C**
		25	**A, A**
		26	**R** HEART = AEHRT
21–22	Refer to Q13–19. Both approaches work for these two questions.	27	**N** CANOE = ACENO
		28	**E** BRACE = ABCER
21	**YZ, AB** Each letter moves forwards two places; each pair is the next two letters in the alphabet.	29	**S** JUMPS = JMPSU
		30	**T** FLUTE = EFLTU
22	**XY, ZA** Each letter moves forwards two places; each pair is the next two letters in the alphabet.	31	**30, 70** The numbers increase by 10 each time.
		32	**1, 4** The numbers increase by 3 each time.
23	**AZ, YX** Each letter moves backwards two places.	33	**25, 30** The numbers increase by 5 each time.
24	**12, 6** Each number decreases by 2.	34	**17, 5** The numbers decrease by 4 each time.
25	**30, 10** Each number decreases by 5.	35	**17, 13** The numbers decrease by 2 each time.
26	**60, 50** Each number decreases by 10.	36	**fire, ice** Ellie dropped a cube of ice into her drink to make it colder.
27	**24, 28** Each number increases by 4.		
28	**G10, H12** The letters move forwards one place. The numbers increase by 2 each time.	37	**box, hole** The dog dug a hole in the garden to bury her bone.
29	**9Y, 7X** The numbers decrease by 2 each time. The letters move backwards one place.	38	**squash, milk** Would you like milk and sugar in your cup of tea?
		39	**worse, better** Doctors treat sick people and make them better.
30	**D5D, F9F** Both letters move forwards one place. The numbers increase by 2 each time.	40	**puppies, kittens** Olivia's tabby cat had five kittens last night!
		41	**d** pond, dishes
		42	**c** traffic, count

Mixed paper 1 (pages 28–31)

		43	**w** pillow, windy
		44	**f** fluff, father
1–5	Try each of the words in the first set of brackets. Do they make sense with any words in the second and third sets of brackets? Only one combination of three words makes sense.	45	**z** buzz, zoo
		46	**MIDDLE**

47 **HIDE** 48 **FATE**
49 **PIECE** 50 **TIRED**
51 **3524** S = 3, N = 5, U = 2, B = 4
52 **7133** T = 7, O = 1, S = 3, S = 3
53 **4127** B = 4, O = 1, U = 2, T = 7
54 **NUTS** 5 = N, 2 = U, 7 = T, 3 = S
55 **SOOT** 3 = S, 1 = O, 1 = O, 7 = T
56 **gear** 57 **pink**
58 **stag** 59 **toil**
60 **foal**

Mixed paper 2 (pages 32–35)

1 **goat, pram** The other words mean a young person.
2 **short, tree** The other words mean to desire or want badly.
3 **start, begin** The other words are all synonyms for end.
4 **uncle, nephew** The other words are all female relations.
5 **give, find** The other words mean to put by or put away for the future.
6 **bend** 'Stoop' and 'bend' both mean to crouch over from an upright position.
7 **soaked** 'Wet' and 'soaked' both mean sodden, usually with water.
8 **mould** To 'shape' and 'mould' both mean to style or form something, like clay.
9 **sore** 'Painful' and 'sore' both mean aching or tender to the touch.
10 **story** 'Tale' and 'story' both mean an account of something.
11 **fine** 'Fine' can mean to be feeling well and healthy; 'fine' can also mean light or thin, like a flimsy material.
12 **graze** A 'graze' can mean a slight injury; to 'graze' can mean to eat (usually grass), or to snack.
13 **tackle** 'Tackle' can refer to rods and reels etc., used in fishing; to 'tackle' can also mean to take on a challenge.
14 **spot** To 'spot' means to recognise something that you are looking for; also, as a noun, it can be a mark or blotch like mud spattered on clothing.
15 **school** A 'school' is a place of learning where children go; to 'school' also means to train or teach.

16

P	L	A	N	E
E		N		V
A	R	G	U	E
R		E		R
L	O	L	L	Y

17

C	R	A	Z	E
	A		E	
T	R	I	B	E
	E		R	
T	R	E	A	T

18

Q	U	E	E	N
U		X		E
I	M	A	G	E
T		C		D
E	N	T	R	Y

19

F		S		F
R	A	N	G	E
A		A		A
M	O	C	K	S
E		K		T

20

Q	U	I	C	K
	P		R	
A	S	H	E	S
	E		A	
S	T	U	M	P

21 **d** raw, dear
22 **n** pod, pine
23 **a** net, stay
24 **d** fin, draft
25 **t** seam, stinks
26 **13** 1 + 3 + 4 + 5 = 13
27 **11** 2 + 5 + 3 + 1 = 11
28 **14** 4 + 3 + 2 + 5 = 14
29 **13** 1 + 5 + 3 + 4 = 13
30 **10** 4 + 3 + 1 + 2 = 10
31 **Then The n**oise from the aeroplanes was incredible.
32 **chin** I looked at my wat**ch in** case we were late.
33 **sour** That dog chase**s our** cat whenever it can.
34 **hand** In the park we played catc**h and** some other games.
35 **term** I will mas**ter m**y fear of heights!
36 ↑ ← ↗ → D = ↑, A = →, R = ↗, E = →
37 ↓ → → ↑ W = ↓, E = →, E = →, D = ↑
38 ↑ → ← ↘ D = ↑, E = →, A = ←, N = ↘
39 **WEAR** ↓ = W, → = E, ← = A, ↗ = R
40 **NEED** ↘ = N, → = E, → = E, ↑ = D

41–43 Use a grid to help you:

L	U	T	O	N		5
B	O	L	T	O	N	1
C	R	A	W	L	E	Y	2
E	X	E	T	E	R		4
D	U	R	H	A	M		3

41 **BOLTON**
42 **DURHAM**
43 **LUTON**

44–46

T	R	A	I	N		5
F	R	A	M	E		3
C	A	L	L	E	R	1
C	O	U	L	D		2
T	O	A	S	T		4

44 **COULD**
45 **TOAST**
46 **light, noise** 'Heavy' is the opposite of 'light' in the same way that 'silence' is the opposite of 'noise'.
47 **hand, foot** A 'hand' is on the end of an 'arm' in the same way a 'foot' is on the end of a 'leg'.
48 **dense, skinny** 'Thick' is similar to 'dense' in the same way 'thin' is a synonym of 'skinny'.
49 **aunt, father** 'Uncle' and 'aunt' are relations that are the male and female version of each other in the same way 'mother' and 'father' are both parents.
50 **cow, sheep** A 'calf' is a young 'cow' in the same way a 'lamb' is a young 'sheep'.
51 **TOUR**
52 **THIN**
53 **EVIL**
54 **RASP**
55 **LOVE**

56–60 Use a chart to help you:

	Round	Oval	Single large stone	Small pips
Peaches	✓		✓	
Cherries	✓		✓	
Blackcurrants	✓			✓
Grapes		✓		✓
Plums		✓	✓	
Lemons		✓		✓

56 plum
57 blackcurrant
58 grape
59 cherry
60 **4** There are 3 in the chart with small pips (blackcurrants, grapes and lemons) plus kiwi fruit = 4.

Mixed paper 3 (pages 36–40)

1 **6201** D = 6, E = 2, A = 0, R = 1
2 **1094** R = 1, A = 0, N = 9, G = 4
3 **41062** G = 4, R = 1, A = 0, D = 6, E = 2
4 **NEAR** 9 = N, 2 = E, 0 = A, R = 1
5 **GREEN** 4 = G, 1 = R, 2 = E, 2 = E, 9 = N

6–8 Use a grid to help you:

L	O	R	R	Y		3
C	A	R				2
V	A	N				5
T	R	A	C	T	O	R	4
B	U	S				1

6 **CAR**
7 **LORRY**
8 **TRACTOR**

9–10 Use a grid to help you:

J	O	K	E	R	3
M	O	U	S	E	5
M	I	X	E	D	4
C	R	A	T	E	1
J	A	D	E	D	2

9 **JOKER**
10 **MIXED**
11 **D Mary attends Willow Tree School.** A, B and C may be true but only D has to be true, given the information.
12 **C Freya has two big brothers.** You know the sister, Freya, is younger than the twins from the information, therefore C is the answer. A, B and D may or may not be true.
13 **A Shaun's new school shoes are black.** You know, from the information, that Shaun's shoes are new and black, therefore A. B is incorrect. C and D may or may not be true.
14–15 You know Joshua has £15. Katya has £9 less than Joshua (15 − 9) so has £6. Callum has £11 more than Katya (6 + 11) so has £17.
14 **£6**
15 **£17**
16 **tow, pull** 'Tow' and 'pull' both mean to drag behind you in a forwards direction.
17 **rash, reckless** 'Rash' and 'reckless' both mean acting quickly in an unthinking and hasty way.
18 **between, amongst** 'Between' and 'amongst' both mean in the middle of a group.
19 **helping, assisting** 'Helping' and 'assisting' both mean aiding or supporting.
20 **caring, compassionate** 'Caring' and 'compassionate' both mean considerate and kind.

21 The sums we did **today** were **easy**.
22 Ethan hit the **ball hard** and straight.
23 He drank his **cup** of **tea** slowly.
24 Mum cut four **large** slices of **cake**.
25 **I** wish **you** were in my class at school.
26 **CRAM**
27 **ITCH**
28 **HOSE**
29 **BEAK**
30 **REEK**
31 **FJ, FI** The first letter is a repeating pattern: FFFFFF. The second letter moves backwards one place.
32 **PO, NM** Each letter moves backwards two places.
33 **EV, FU** The first letter moves forwards one place. The second letter moves backwards one place.
34 **TO, YN** The first letter is a repeating pattern: TYTYTY. The second letter moves backwards one place.
35 **KL, MN** Each letter moves forwards two places.
36–40 Use a grid to help you:

	Dark hair	Fair hair	Green eyes	Brown eyes
Maisy	✓		✓	
Nihal	✓			✓
Nadia		✓		✓
Harry		✓	✓	

36 **Nadia**
37 **Harry**
38 **Nihal**
39 **Maisy**
40 **3** Harry and Nadia and Anna have fair hair, so 3.
41 **DIN** dinner
42 **TEN** lightened
43 **SUN** sunbathe
44 **RAN** entrance
45 **RAG** garage
46 **gems** There is no 'M' in GARDENS.
47 **wool** There is only one 'O' in PILLOWS.
48 **urge** There is no 'U' in TIGHTER.
49 **faze** There is no 'Z' in FLAMES.
50 **chop** There is no 'P' in BLOTCH.
51 **FARM**

1	2					3	4
J	U	S	T		R	A	M	P

(correction)

1	2		
J	U	S	T

		3	4
R	A	M	P

1	2		
F	A	I	R

		3	4
W	O	R	M

52 **JOKE**

1	2		
L	I	O	N

		3	4
S	T	E	P

1	2		
J	O	I	N

		3	4
K	E	P	T

53 **SOFT**

		3	4
H	E	M	S

1	2		
G	U	L	F

		3	4
R	I	F	T

1	2		
S	O	N	G

54 **CALM**

	2	3	
B	O	A	T

1			4
S	I	N	K

	2	3	
H	A	L	F

1			4
C	R	A	M

55 **POLE**

	2	3	4
B	O	W	L

			1
E	A	C	H

	2	3	4
M	O	L	E

			1
D	U	M	P

56 strong, delicate
57 serious, foolish
58 life, death
59 under, over
60 sweet, sour

Mixed paper 4 (pages 41–44)

1 **BLOW**
2 **ANSWER**
3 **BORED**
4 **FOR**
5 **WISE**
6 hinge, oiled
7 keys, drain
8 plays, piano
9 front, green
10 rough, bathe
11 **SOUR**
12 **FALL**
13 **BOOT**
14 **NEAT**
15 **BOND**
16 playroom
17 understand
18 jobless

19 **managed**
20 **handsome**
21 **g p w d** V = g, I = p, S = w, A = d
22 **w d w m** S = w, A = d, S = w, H = m
23 **SHIN** w = S, m = H, p = I, b = N
24 **VAIN** g = V, d = A, p = I, b = N
25 **HISS** m = H, p = I, w = S, w = S
26 **M** SMILE = EILMS
27 **R** CRAZE = ACERZ
28 **T** BUILT = BILTU
29 **I** FINCH = CFHIN
30 **S** JUMPS = JMPSU
31 **XY** Each letter moves forwards two places.
32 **RQ** Each letter moves backwards two places.
33 **MO** Each letter moves forwards four places.
34 **MN** Each letter moves forwards two places.
35 **TT** Each letter moves backwards two places.
36 **A Betsy is a terrier.** From the information, it has to be A. B, C and D may or may not be true.
37 **B Maidstone is in the south-east of England.** A, C and D are likely to be true but A has to be true given the information.
38 **C Daniel wears his read and grey uniform to school.** If Daniel's school uniform is red and grey, it must be true that he wears it to school.
39 **20** 9 + 11 = 20
40 **14** 7 + 7 = 14
41 **15** 5 × 3 = 15
42 **14** 4 + 3 + 5 + 2 = 14
43 **4** (3 + 5) ÷ 2 = 4
44 **10** (4 ÷ 2) × 5 = 10
45 **6** (5 + 4) − 3 = 6
46 **story, fable** The other words are all synonyms of joke or prank.
47 **hush, silence** The other words are all synonyms of quick.
48 **spade, fork** The other words are all precious jewels.
49 **hint, clue** The other words all mean the part behind or at the back, not at the front.
50 **icy, freezing** The other words all mean very hot.
51 **t** mint, table; stout, tear
52 **d** rind, durable; sword, despair
53 **g** fling, garage; bearing, gone
54 **p** jump, pear; shrimp, party
55 **a** arena, azure; pizza, apple
56 **strain, stress** 'Strain' and 'stress' both mean pressure, tension or anxiety.
57 **snap, break** 'Snap' and 'break' both mean to crack or shatter.
58 **find, discover** 'Find' and 'discover' both mean to locate or detect.
59 **race, sprint** 'Race' and 'sprint' both mean to run quickly.
60 **spell, charm** 'Spell' and 'charm' both mean an enchantment.

Mixed paper 5 (pages 45–48)

1 **PEARL**
2 **SQUID**
3 **BLACK**
4 **GRAIN**
5 **SLIME**
6 **STOP**
7 **MALE**
8 **TEAR**
9 **SLIP**
10 **DONE**
11–15 Three of the words begin with 'F' which therefore is 5 and HARM = 1634. FEET has double 'EE' which means that FEET = 5228. From this you can work out all the letters and their codes.
11 5642
12 1634
13 5682
14 5228
15 **FARM** 5 = F, 6 = A, 3 = R, 4 = M
16–20 Will is directly above Jack, Fin is below May so therefore Ali has to be 2. If Ali is to the right of May, then May = 1, Fin = 4. Therefore, Will = 3 and Jack = 6.
16 **3**
17 **6**
18 **1**
19 **4**
20 **2**
21 **inner, outer** 'Inner' means inside whereas 'outer' means outside.
22 **evening, morning** 'Evening' is the end of the day whereas 'morning' is the beginning.
23 **dull, bright** 'Dull' means not shiny whereas 'bright' means shiny or glossy.
24 **useless, useful** 'Useless' means hopeless or inadequate whereas 'useful' means worthwhile or handy.
25 **common, rare** 'Common' means normal or usual whereas 'rare' means unusual or uncommon.
26 **rue** The pattern is to remove the first letter of the first word.
27 **stew** The pattern is to remove the last two letters of the first word, 'ab', and replace them with 'ew'.
28 **dear** The pattern is to remove the first letter of the first word, 'b', and replace it with 'd'.
29 **fable** The pattern is to place the letter 'f' at the front of the first word.
30 **all** The pattern is to remove the first two letters and the final three ('ing'), leaving only the third, fourth and fifth letters of the first word.
31 **20** 2 × 10 = 20
32 **6** (3 + 5) − 2 = 6
33 **3** (3 + 2 + 10) ÷ 5 = 3

34 **2** (10 ÷ 2) − 3 = 2
35 **12** (10 − 3) + 5 = 12
36 **suitable, proper**
37 **stay, remain**
38 **still, motionless**
39 **discover, find**
40 **extend, enlarge**
41 **TALE, LATE**
42 **FELT, LEFT**
43 **RISE, SIRE**
44 **FLAIR, FRAIL**
45 **STALE, LEAST**
46 **roof** A 'roof' is part of all houses whereas the others may or may not be present.
47 **rails** Trains have to run on 'rails', so a 'station' must have 'rails' as it is where trains stop.
48 **Christmas** 'Christmas' is on 'December' 25th. It does not necessarily have cold weather as in other parts of the world December is a hot month.
49 **a football** The game football has to be played with 'a football'.
50 **eyes** 'Eyes' are part of the lamb's body that all lambs have.
51 **m d f e** B = m, A = d, R = f, N = e
52 **RAIN** f = R, d = A, w = I, e = N
53 **2349** L = 2, A = 3, N = 4, E = 9
54 **HEED** 7 = H, 9 = E, 9 = E, 5 = D
55 **MESH** £ = M, + = E, ? = S, & = H
56 **ED, CB** Each letter moves backwards two places.
57 **EF, FG** The first letters are a repeating pattern: EFEFEF. The second letters are in alphabetical order, moving forwards one place each time.
58 **ZA, BC** Each letter moves forward two places. The first answer is 'ZA' and the second answer 'BC' as, when you reach the end of the alphabet, you go back to the beginning with 'A' again and so on.
59 **XW, VU** Each letter moves backwards two places.
60 **BC, DE** Each letter moves forwards two places, so the letters are in alphabetical order.

Mixed paper 6 (pages 49–52)

1 **FIRE**
2 **FLOW**
3 **REAP**
4 **STEER**
5 **SPARE**
6 **water** waterproof, watertight, waterlogged, watermelon
7 **brain** brainwave, brainwash, brainstorm, brainbox
8 **after** afternoon, aftercare, aftertaste, afterthought
9 **wind** windswept, windmill, windsurf, windscreen
10 **horse** horsepower, horsefly, horseback, horseshoe
11–15 Use a chart to help you:

1 used	2	3	4	5	6 my peg	7	8	9 Jade	10 Sophia
11 used	12	13	14	15	16 Fiona	17	18	19	20

If I am using 6, then opposite my peg is 16 (Fiona). Sophia is the end of the top row; as 1 is taken, therefore 10. Next to 10 is 9 (Jade). The peg opposite Sophia's (10) is 20. The peg opposite Jade's (9) is 19.

11 **16**
12 **10**
13 **9**
14 **20**
15 **19**
16 **11** 2 + 3 + 1 = 5 = 11
17 **12** 1 + 2 + 4 + 5 = 12
18 **10** 1 + 3 + 4 + 2 = 10
19 **13** 5 + 3 + 3 + 2 = 13
20 **10** 2 + 3 + 4 + 1 = 10
21 **bake** There is no 'e' in BACKING.
22 **dead** There is no 'a' in DWINDLE.
23 **teas** There is no 's' in TRAINED.
24 **song** There is no 'o' in PLEASING.
25 **germ** There is no 'e' in FRAMING.
26 **e** bled, niece
27 **s** grow, seals
28 **a** bout, heard
29 **r** tail, first
30 **n** sail, snows
31 **comfort, succour**
32 **path, track**
33 **snug, cosy**
34 **cool, unflappable**
35 **soak, drench**
36 **/ D v h** F = /, A = D, K = v, E = h
37 **N h 3 7** B = N, E = h, S = 3, T = 7
38 **BASK** N = B, D = A, 3 = S, v = K
39 **RAKE** ^ = R, D = A, v = K, h = E
40 **FEAR** / = F, h = E, D = A, ^ = R
41 **30, 45** The numbers increase by 5 each time.
42 **3, 15** The numbers increase by 3 each time.
43 **D10, C12** The letters move backwards by one place each time. The numbers increase by 2 each time.
44 **3Y, 4X** The numbers increase by 1 each time. The letters move backwards one place each time.

45 **4n, 6p** The numbers increase by 1 each time. The letters move forward one place.

46–48 Use a chart to help you:

R	U	N	N	Y	5
R	A	P	I	D	1
R	E	L	A	Y	2
R	O	U	N	D	4
R	I	S	K	Y	3

46 RELAY
47 ROUND
48 RUNNY

49–50 Use a chart to help you:

M	O	N	D	A	Y			2
T	U	E	S	D	A	Y		6
W	E	D	N	E	S	D	A	Y	7
T	H	U	R	S	D	A	Y		5
F	R	I	D	A	Y			1
S	A	T	U	R	D	A	Y		3
S	U	N	D	A	Y			4

49 Wednesday
50 Monday
51 dark 'Light' means bright or shining whereas 'dark' means without light.
52 out 'In' means inside something whereas 'out' means outside something.
53 future 'Past' refers to something that has happened whereas 'future' is yet to come.
54 right 'Left' and 'right' are opposites as they refer to different or opposing sides of something.
55 untie 'Fasten' means to attach or tie whereas 'untie' is to detach or undo something.

56

G	R	A	V	E
A		Z		M
T	H	U	M	B
E		R		E
S	T	E	E	R

57

T	R	U	S	T
	O		U	
S	W	E	P	T
	A		E	
S	N	A	R	L

58

M	I	T	R	E
O		R		N
P	L	A	N	T
E		D		E
S	P	E	A	R

59

A		L		Y
B	L	A	M	E
O		S		A
V	O	T	E	R
E		S		N

60

J	U	M	P	S
	N		R	
E	D	G	E	S
	E		E	
B	R	I	N	G

Give the next two pairs of letters in the following sequences. The alphabet has been written out to help you.

A B C D E F G H I J K L M N O P Q R S T U V W X Y Z

Example	CQ	DP	EQ	FP	GQ	HP
13	AB	CD	EF	GH	___	___
14	FG	IJ	LM	OP	___	___
15	AC	EG	IK	MO	___	___
16	ZX	VT	RP	NL	___	___
17	DA	GB	DC	GD	___	___
18	UF	VG	WH	XI	___	___
19	ZV	YT	XR	WP	___	___
20	KN	IJ	GN	EJ	___	___

Here, the letters in each pair are working separately.

Example	RS	TU	VW	XY	ZA	BC
21	QR	ST	UV	WX	___	___
22	PQ	RS	TU	VW	___	___
23	IH	GF	ED	CB	___	___

Treat the alphabet like a continuous line – XYZAB and BAZYX, and so on.

Give the missing two numbers and/or letters in the following sequences.

Example	2	4	6	8	10	12
24	16	14	___	10	8	___
25	___	25	20	15	___	5
26	___	___	40	30	20	10
27	16	20	___	___	32	36

Look for the pattern between the numbers.

In these questions, find the patterns for the numbers and the letters separately.

28	C2	D4	E6	F8	___	___
29	13A	11Z	___	___	5W	3V
30	C3C	___	E7E	___	G11G	H13H

Mixed paper 1

Complete the following sentences by selecting the most sensible word from each group of words given in the brackets. Underline the words selected.

Example The (<u>children</u>, boxes, foxes) carried the (houses, <u>books</u>, steps) home from the (greengrocer, <u>library</u>, factory).

1 When the (circus, bus, rain) came to town last month, Dad bought (groceries, paper, tickets) and we all went one (evening, year, minute).

2 Our little cat had six (puppies, lambs, kittens) a few (weeks, seconds, minutes) ago and they are now (reading, barking, playing) as their eyes have opened and their legs are stronger.

3 Big (cars, supermarkets, hotels) have pumps that sell (fuel, swimming pools, bicycles) as well as household things and (food, factories, fires).

4 The (noise, taste, smell) of the (roadworks, posters, lights) is making my head (dance, sing, ache).

5 On her (lap, chair, birthday) Amy received six (helpings, cards, berries) and two (rabbits, tissues, parcels) in the post.

Find the three-letter word that can be added to the letters in capitals to make a new word. The new word will complete the sentence sensibly. Write the three-letter word.

Example The cat sprang onto the MO.   <u>USE</u>

6 I was given a new notepad with coloured PR for my birthday.

7 We will go for a run LR this afternoon.

8 Sonia's cat had three KITS.

9 Ice made the path dangerous and SPERY.

10 As it was so wet, our LAWNMR got stuck and would not cut.

Which one letter can be added to the front of all of these words to make new words?

Example   ___are   ___at   ___rate   ___all   <u>c</u>

11   ___often   ___ink   ___inner   ___elfish   ___

12   ___erring   ___anger   ___ours   ___ate   ___

13   ___order   ___lasting   ___rainy   ___lame   ___

14   ___lash   ___alter   ___lung   ___right   ___

15   ___an   ___omit   ___alley   ___ague   ___

Stefan and Robert both support local football teams. Robert supports a team who play in a red strip. Stefan's team plays in blue. The boys kept a chart of the number of goals scored month by month. Using the chart, answer the questions below.

	October	November	December	January	February	March
RED	5	9	20	12	11	13
BLUE	7	11	9	14	17	13

16   How many goals were scored in February, altogether? _____

17   How many goals did Robert's team score in the first three months? _____

18   How many goals did Stefan's team score in the final three months? _____

19   In which month were the most goals scored? _____

20   Whose team scored more goals altogether? _____

Look at these groups of words.

        A   B   C
Languages   Colours   Trees

Choose the correct group for each of the words below. Write in the letter.

21   French ___   yellow ___

22   beech ___   red ___

23   purple ___   black ___

24   cherry ___   oak ___

25   Greek ___   Spanish ___

If the letters in the following words are arranged in alphabetical order, which letter comes fourth?

26 HEART ____

27 CANOE ____

28 BRACE ____

29 JUMPS ____

30 FLUTE ____

Give the missing two numbers in the following sequences.

Example	2	4	6	8	<u>10</u>	<u>12</u>
31	____	40	50	60	____	80
32	____	____	7	10	13	16
33	15	20	____	____	35	40
34	25	21	____	13	9	____
35	19	____	15	____	11	9

Change one word so that the sentence makes sense. Underline the word you are taking out and write your new word on the line.

Example I waited in line to buy a <u>book</u> to see the film. <u>ticket</u>

36 Ellie dropped a cube of fire into her drink to make it colder. ____

37 The dog dug a box in the garden to bury her bone. ____

38 Would you like squash and sugar in your cup of tea? ____

39 Doctors treat sick people and make them worse. ____

40 Olivia's tabby cat had five puppies last night! ____

Find the letter that will end the first word and start the second word.

Example drow (<u>n</u>) ought

41 pon (__) ishes

42 traffi (__) ount

43 pillo (__) indy

44 fluf (__) ather

45 buz (__) oo

Find a word that is similar in meaning to the word in capital letters and that rhymes with the second word.

Example CABLE   tyre   <u>WIRE</u>

46 CENTRE   fiddle   _____
47 CONCEAL   wide   _____
48 DESTINY   wait   _____
49 PART   fleece   _____
50 WEARY   hired   _____

The code for BUTTONS is 4 2 7 7 1 5 3. Encode each of these words using the same code.

51 SNUB _____   52 TOSS _____   53 BOUT _____

Decode these words using the same code as above.

54 5 2 7 3 _____   55 3 1 1 7 _____

Underline the one word in each group that **can be made** from the letters of the word in capital letters.

Example CHAMPION   camping   notch   peach   cramp   <u>chimp</u>

56 STRANGE   stun   gear   guns   tree   gain
57 PUMPKIN   pink   pack   inky   sunk   king
58 GHASTLY   cast   list   gale   stag   hate
59 PISTOLS   kiss   slow   plus   also   toil
60 FLAVOUR   rave   furs   love   foal   vale

Mixed paper 2

Underline the two words that are the odd ones out in the following group of words.

Example   black   <u>king</u>   purple   green   <u>house</u>

1 kid   goat   youngster   child   pram
2 short   long   pine   yearn   tree
3 stop   start   halt   begin   finish
4 sister   aunt   uncle   nephew   grandmother
5 give   store   hoard   find   keep

Underline the word in the brackets that is closest in meaning to the word in capitals.

Example   UNHAPPY   (unkind   death   laughter   <u>sad</u>   friendly)

6 STOOP   (crawl   carry   tire   bend   fold)
7 WET   (soaked   rain   dry   desert   soften)
8 SHAPE   (square   mould   sign   rotten   solid)
9 PAINFUL   (sorry   sore   cry   grief   uneasy)
10 TALE   (story   moral   end   rhyme   poem)

Underline the one word in brackets that will go equally well with both the pairs of words outside the brackets.

Example   rush, attack   cost, fee   (price, hasten, strike, <u>charge</u>, money)

11 well, healthy   thin, light   (slim, skinny, fine, delicate, flimsy)
12 small cut, scrape   eat grass, snack   (chew, slice, plaster, meal, graze)
13 fishing kit, equipment   face up to, handle   (rod, gear, tackle, angle, block)
14 notice, see   stain, mark   (spot, view, blotch, spill, perceive)
15 place of learning, education   coach, instruct   (train, school, academy, college, tutor)

Fill in the crosswords so that all the given words are included. You have been given one letter as a clue in each crossword.

16 PLANE / EVERY / ARGUE / ANGEL / LOLLY / PEARL (clue: L)

17 TREAT / CRAZE / ZEBRA / TRIBE / RARER (clue: Z)

18 ENTRY / IMAGE / QUITE / QUEEN / NEEDY / EXACT (clue: I)

19 FEAST / FRAME / MOCKS / SNACK / RANGE (clue: G)

20 ASHES / CREAM / QUICK / STUMP / UPSET (clue: H)

Move one letter from the first word to the second word to make two new words.

Example   hunt   sip   <u>hut</u>   <u>snip</u>

21   draw   ear   _____   _____
22   pond   pie   _____   _____
23   neat   sty   _____   _____
24   find   raft _____   _____
25   steam sinks _____   _____

If s = 1, t = 2, a = 3, l = 4 and e = 5, what are the totals of these words?

26 sale ____   27 teas ____
28 late ____   29 seal ____
30 last ____

Write the four-letter word hidden at the end of one word and the beginning of the next word in each sentence. The order of the letters may not be changed.

Example We had bats and balls.   sand

31 The noise from the aeroplanes was incredible.   _____

32 I looked at my watch in case we were late.   _____

33 That dog chases our cat whenever it can.   _____

34 In the park we played catch and some other games.   _____

35 I will master my fear of heights!   _____

The code for WANDER is ↓ ← ↖ ↑ → ↗. Encode each of these words using the same code.

36 DARE _____   37 WEED _____   38 DEAN _____

Decode these words using the same code as above.

39 ↓ → ← ↗ _____   40 ↖ → → ↑ _____

LUTON   BOLTON   CRAWLEY   EXETER   DURHAM

If these towns are put into alphabetical order, which comes:

41 first? _____   42 third? _____   43 last? _____

TRAIN   FRAME   CALLER   COULD   TOAST

If these words are put into alphabetical order, which comes:

44 second? _____   45 fourth? _____

Complete the following sentences in the best way by choosing one word from each set of brackets.

Example Tall is to (tree, short, colour) as narrow is to (thin, white, wide).

46 Heavy is to (light, difficult, wood) as silence is to (peace, noise, mark).

47 Arm is to (finger, body, hand) as leg is to (knee, sock, foot).

48 Thick is to (dense, slender, high) as thin is to (low, variety, skinny).

49 Uncle is to (aunt, brother, grandfather) as mother is to (baby, home, father).

50 Calf is to (field, cow, bull) as lamb is to (sheep, meat, fleece).

Rearrange the letters in capitals to make another word. The new word has something to do with the first two words or phrases.

Example	spot	soil	SAINT	<u>STAIN</u>
51	trip	outing	ROUT	_____
52	slim	skinny	HINT	_____
53	wicked	harmful	LIVE	_____
54	file	grate	SPAR	_____
55	adore	worship	VOLE	_____

Peaches, cherries and blackcurrants are round.
Grapes, plums and lemons are oval.
Peaches, cherries and plums have a single large stone.
The others have small pips.

56 Which fruit is oval with a large stone? _____

57 Which fruit is round with small pips? _____

58 Which fruit, besides a lemon, is oval with small pips? _____

59 Which fruit, besides a peach, is round with a large stone? _____

60 If a kiwi is oval with small pips, how many fruits, now, altogether have small pips? _____

Now go to the Progress Chart to record your score! Total

Mixed paper 3

The code for DANGER is 6 0 9 4 2 1. Encode these words.

1 DEAR _____   2 RANG _____   3 GRADE _____

Decode these words using the same code as above.

4 9 2 0 1 _____   5 4 1 2 2 9 _____

    LORRY   CAR   VAN   TRACTOR   BUS

If these words are put into alphabetical order, which comes:

6 second? _____   7 third? _____   8 fourth? _____

    JOKER   MOUSE   MIXED   CRATE   JADED

If these words are put into alphabetical order, which comes:

9 third? _____   10 fourth? _____

Read the first two statements and then underline the one option that must be true.

11 Mary is in Class 5. Class 5 is one of the classes at Willow Tree School.

    A Elise, Mary's friend, is also in Class 5.

    B Class 5 is next to Class 4.

    C Mary likes school.

    D Mary attends Willow Tree School.

12 Aidan and Ryan are twins. The twins have a baby sister, Freya.

    A Ryan is the older of the twins.

    B Aidan loves babies.

    C Freya has two big brothers.

    D Aidan and Ryan look after Freya.

13 Shaun has a new pair of school shoes. Shaun's school insists on pupils wearing black shoes.

   A Shaun's new school shoes are black.

   B Shaun's new school shoes are brown.

   C Shaun's shoes are a little bit tight.

   D Shaun walks to school in his new shoes.

Callum has £11 more savings than Katya, who has £9 less savings than Joshua, who has £15 savings.

14 How much does Katya have? ____

15 How much does Callum have? ____

Underline the two words in each line that are most similar in type or meaning.

Example <u>dear</u>   pleasant   poor   extravagant   <u>expensive</u>

16 toe   tow   leg   pull   push

17 sensible   rash   vibrant   reckless   alive

18 between   over   under   inside   amongst

19 helping   organise   correct   assisting   wrong

20 cruel   dirty   caring   simple   compassionate

Find and underline the two words that need to change places for each sentence to make sense.

Example She went to <u>letter</u> the <u>write</u>.

21 The sums we did easy were today.

22 Ethan hit the hard ball and straight.

23 He drank his tea of cup slowly.

24 Mum cut four cake slices of large.

25 You wish I were in my class at school.

Remove one letter from the word in capital letters to leave a new word. The meaning of the new word is given in the clue.

Example AUNT   an insect   <u>ANT</u>

26 CREAM   overfill   _____

27 WITCH   tickle   _____

28 HOUSE   pipe   _____

29 BREAK   bill   _____

30 CREEK   smell   _____

Give the next two pairs of letters in the following sequences. The alphabet has been written out to help you.

A B C D E F G H I J K L M N O P Q R S T U V W X Y Z

Example CQ   DP   EQ   FP   <u>GQ</u>   <u>HP</u>

31 FN   FM   FL   FK   ___   ___

32 XW   VU   TS   RQ   ___   ___

33 AZ   BY   CX   DW   ___   ___

34 TS   YR   TQ   YP   ___   ___

35 CD   EF   GH   IJ   ___   ___

Maisy and Nihal have dark hair.
Nadia and Harry have fair hair.
Maisy and Harry have green eyes.
Nihal and Nadia have brown eyes.

36 Who has fair hair and brown eyes?   _____

37 Who has fair hair and green eyes?   _____

38 Who has dark hair and brown eyes?   _____

39 Who has dark hair and green eyes?   _____

40 Their friend Anna has fair hair and blue eyes. How many now have fair hair?   _____

Find the three-letter word that can be added to the letters in capitals to make a new word. The new word will complete the sentence sensibly. Write the three-letter word.

Example The cat sprang onto the MO. <u>USE</u>

41 He was sent to change his T-shirt and wash his hands before NER. _____

42 As the sun rose, the sky LIGHED and it became morning. _____

43 Emily likes to BATHE on the beach in the summer. _____

44 The ENTCE to the stadium was packed with people trying to get in. _____

45 She parked the car carefully in the GAE and closed the doors. _____

Underline the one word in each group that **cannot be made** from the letters of the word in capital letters.

Example	STATIONERY	stone	tyres	ration	<u>nation</u>	noisy
46	GARDENS	gems	rang	dens	snag	near
47	PILLOWS	slip	wool	slop	slow	soil
48	TIGHTER	grit	rite	tier	urge	tire
49	FLAMES	same	slam	safe	fame	faze
50	BLOTCH	loch	both	clot	chop	bolt

Look at the first group of three words. The word in the middle has been made from the two other words. Complete the second group of three words in the same way, making a new word in the middle of the group.

Example	PAIN	IN<u>TO</u>	TOOK	ALSO	<u>SOON</u>	ONLY
51	JUST	JUMP	RAMP	FAIR	_____	WORM
52	LION	LIST	STEP	JOIN	_____	KEPT
53	HEMS	GUMS	GULF	RIFT	_____	SONG
54	BOAT	SOAK	SINK	HALF	_____	CRAM
55	BOWL	HOWL	EACH	MOLE	_____	DUMP

Underline the pair of words most opposite in meaning.

Example cup, mug coffee, milk <u>hot, cold</u>

56 feeble, weak <u>strong, delicate</u> silver, gold

57 idiotic, stupid serious, foolish <u>sensible, thinking</u>

58 <u>life, death</u> soon, presently bind, bird

59 bizarre, strange normal, ordinary <u>under, over</u>

60 <u>sweet, sour</u> drizzle, rain made, maid

Mixed paper 4

Find a word that is opposite in meaning to the word in capital letters and that rhymes with the second word.

Example QUICK   grow   <u>SLOW</u>

1 SUCK   foe   _____
2 QUESTION   dancer   _____
3 INTERESTED   afford   _____
4 AGAINST   paw   _____
5 FOOLISH   buys   _____

Rearrange the muddled words in capital letters so that each sentence makes sense.

Example There are sixty SNODCES <u>seconds</u> in a UTMINE <u>minute</u>.

6 The GNEHI _____ of my bedroom door needs to be LOIDE _____ as it is really squeaky.

7 Poor Soolin accidentally dropped her SEYK _____ down a RDANI _____ on the street.

8 She LAYSP _____ the IANPO _____ really tunefully and well.

9 The NTRFO _____ door to our house is painted NGERE _____.

10 The sea was too GHROU _____ to THBAE _____ safely.

Change the first word into the last word by changing one letter at a time and making a new, different word in the middle.

Example CASE   <u>CASH</u>   LASH

11 SOUP   _____   TOUR
12 CALL   _____   FILL
13 BOAT   _____   BOOK
14 NEAR   _____   NEWT
15 BAND   _____   FOND

Underline two words, one from each group, that go together to form a new word. The word in the first group always comes first.

Example   (hand, green, for)   (light, house, sure)

16 (play, walk, ring)   (toy, king, room)

17 (in, under, up)   (saw, stand, near)

18 (still, job, all)   (so, more, less)

19 (man, very, some)   (thin, aged, old)

20 (foot, hand, toe)   (full, some, dell)

The code for VANISH is g d b p w m. Encode each of these words using the same code.

21 VISA _____   22 SASH _____

Decode these words using the same code as above.

23 w m p b _____   24 g d p b _____

25 m p w w _____

If the letters in the following words are arranged in alphabetical order, which letter comes fourth?

26 SMILE ___
27 CRAZE ___
28 BUILT ___
29 FINCH ___
30 JUMPS ___

Fill in the missing letters. The alphabet has been written out to help you.

A B C D E F G H I J K L M N O P Q R S T U V W X Y Z

Example AB is to CD as PQ is to <u>RS</u>.

31 HI is to JK as VW is to ___.

32 PO is to NM as TS is to ___.

33 AC is to EG as IK is to ___.

34 WX is to YZ as KL is to ___.

35 ZZ is to XX as VV is to ___.

Read the first two statements and then underline the one option that must be true.

36 Betsy is a terrier. Terriers are a type of dog.

   A Betsy is a dog.

   B Betsy is a fierce dog.

   C Betsy has a blue collar.

   D Betsy goes for walks in the park.

37 Maidstone is a town in Kent. Kent is a county in the south-east of England.

   A Maidstone is an important town.

   B Maidstone is in the south-east of England.

   C There are many towns in Kent.

   D Kent is near London.

38 Daniel's school jumper is red. Daniel's school uniform is red and grey.

   A Daniel's school trousers have pockets.

   B Daniel likes his school uniform.

   C Daniel wears his red and grey uniform to school.

   D Daniel left his red jumper on the bus.

39 If Zachary was 11 when his cousin, Grace, was born and she is 9 now,

   how old is Zachary? _____

40 If Jess was 7 when her cousin, Saul, was born and he is 7 now, how old is Jess? _____

If $u = 2$, $w = 5$, $y = 3$ and $z = 4$, find the value of the following calculations.

   41 $w \times y =$ _____

   42 $z + y + w + u =$ _____

   43 $(y + w) \div u =$ _____

   44 $(z \div u) \times w =$ _____

   45 $(w + z) - y =$ _____

Underline the two words that are the odd ones out in the following group of words.

Example   black   king   purple   green   house

46   story   jest   joke   fable   jape
47   rapid   fast   hush   swift   silence
48   diamond   ruby   sapphire   spade   fork
49   hint   hind   clue   back   rear
50   sizzling   burning   icy   freezing   fiery

Find the letter that will complete both pairs of words, ending the first word and starting the second. The same letter must be used for both pairs of words.

Example   mea (t) able   fi (t) ub

51   min (__) able   stou (__) ear
52   rin (__) urable   swor (__) espair
53   flin (__) arage   bearin (__) one
54   jum (__) ear   shrim (__) arty
55   aren (__) zure   pizz (__) pple

Underline the two words, one from each group, that are the closest in meaning.

Example   (race, shop, start)   (finish, begin, end)

56   (strain, freeze, bite)   (bounce, stress, melt)
57   (snap, crackle, pop)   (break, plod, mount)
58   (find, fine, fire)   (discover, lose, merge)
59   (choose, race, clear)   (cheer, sprint, claim)
60   (spell, bout, period)   (chart, chief, charm)

Mixed paper 5

Add one letter to the word in capital letters to make a new word. The meaning of the new word is given in the clue.

Example PLAN   simple   <u>PLAIN</u>

1. EARL   gem from an oyster   _____
2. QUID   sea animal   _____
3. BACK   dark colour   _____
4. GAIN   wheat, barley   _____
5. SLIM   mucus, goo   _____

Rearrange the letters in capitals to make another word. The new word has something to do with the first two words or phrases.

Example spot   soil   SAINT   <u>STAIN</u>

6. halt   stay   POTS   _____
7. man   boy   LAME   _____
8. hole   split   RATE   _____
9. slide   error   LIPS   _____
10. complete   finished   NODE   _____

These words have been written in code, but the codes are not written under the right words. Match the right code to each word given below.

FAME	HARM	FATE	FEET
1 6 3 4	5 2 2 8	5 6 8 2	5 6 4 2

11. FAME _____
12. HARM _____
13. FATE _____
14. FEET _____

15. Using the same code, decode 5 6 3 4. _____

School lockers are in groups of six, as in the diagram.

LEFT	TOP	RIGHT
1	2	3
4	5 JUAN	6

BOTTOM

Will's locker was directly above Jack's. May's locker was not next to or right above Juan's. Fin's locker was on the bottom row directly below May's locker. Ali's locker was next to and to the right of May's locker.

From the information, work out which child has which number locker.

16 Will _3_   17 Jack _6_
18 May   _1_   19 Fin   _4_
20 Ali   _2_

Underline the two words, one from each group, that are the most opposite in meaning.

Example (dawn, <u>early</u>, wake)   (<u>late</u>, stop, sunrise)

21 (<u>inner</u>, middle, there)   (side, <u>outer</u>, centre)
22 (<u>evening</u>, noon, day)   (mourning, awning, <u>morning</u>)
23 (<u>dull</u>, thick, brassy)   (cloudy, gloomy, <u>bright</u>)
24 (<u>useless</u>, handy, bright)   (<u>useful</u>, worthless, pointless)
25 (common, under, <u>extra</u>)   (beneath, <u>rare</u>, more)

Change the first word of the third pair in the same way as the other pairs to give a new word.

Example bind, hind   bare, hare   but, <u>hut</u>

26 pair, air   pram, ram   true, _rue_
27 crab, crew   grab, grew   stab, _stew_
28 bean, dean   bell, dell   bear, _dear_
29 inch, finch   east, feast   able, _fable_
30 clowning, own   braiding, aid   stalling, _all_

If m = 2, n = 5, p = 3 and q = 10, find the value of the following calculations.

31 m × q = _____

32 (p + n) − m = _____

33 (p + m + q) ÷ n = _____

34 (q ÷ m) − p = _____

35 (q − p) + n = _____

Underline the pair of words most similar in meaning.

Example come, go   <u>roams, wanders</u>   fear, fare

36 idle, active	dream, wake	suitable, proper
37 fasten, release	stay, remain	into, onto
38 still, motionless	quiet, noise	never, sometimes
39 hide, seek	discover, find	appear, go
40 pretend, real	climb, descend	extend, enlarge

Underline the two words in each line that are made from the same letters.

Example TAP   PET   <u>TEA</u>   POT   <u>EAT</u>

41 SEAS	TALE	SALE	LATE	TEAS
42 TELL	FELL	LEAF	FELT	LEFT
43 SURE	FURS	RISE	FIRS	SIRE
44 FLAIR	FRAIL	FAILS	SAILS	FAIRS
45 STALE	STALL	SEALS	LASTS	LEAST

Choose the word or phrase that makes each sentence true.

Example A LIBRARY always has (posters, a carpet, <u>books</u>, DVDs, stairs).

46 A HOUSE always has a (garden, roof, person, flagpole, cat).

47 A TRAIN STATION always has (a road, a freight train, a guard, rails, four platforms).

48 DECEMBER always has (cold weather, Christmas, Mum's birthday, snow, floods).

49 A FOOTBALL MATCH always has (a football, grass, crowds, linesmen, a stadium).

50 A LAMB always has (white fleece, long tail, eyes, sheepdog, horns).

51 If the code for BRAIN is m f d w e, encode BARN.

52 Using the same code as for BRAIN, decode f d w e.

53 If the code for HANDLE is 7 3 4 5 2 9, encode LANE.

54 Using the same code as for HANDLE, decode 7 9 9 5.

55 If the code for SHAME is ? & % £ +, decode £ + ? &.

Give the next two pairs of letters in the following sequences. The alphabet has been written out to help you.

A B C D E F G H I J K L M N O P Q R S T U V W X Y Z

Example	RS	TU	VW	XY	ZA	BC
56	ML	KJ	IH	GF	___	___
57	EB	FC	ED	FE	___	___
58	RS	TU	VW	XY	___	___
59	FE	DC	BA	ZY	___	___
60	TU	VW	XY	ZA	___	___

Mixed paper 6

Rearrange the letters in capitals to make another word. The new word has something to do with the first two words or phrases.

Example	spot	soil	SAINT	STAIN
1	burning	blaze	RIFE	_____
2	stream	pour	WOLF	_____
3	harvest	gather	PEAR	_____
4	drive	guide	TREES	_____
5	extra	pardon	SPEAR	_____

Find a word that can be put in front of each of the following words to make new, compound words.

Example	cast	fall	ward	pour	down
6	proof	tight	logged	melon	_____
7	wave	wash	storm	box	_____
8	noon	care	taste	thought	_____
9	swept	mill	surf	screen	_____
10	power	fly	back	shoe	_____

In a changing room there are twenty pegs in two rows numbered 1 to 10 and 11 to 20. Number 1 is opposite number 11, 2 is opposite 12 and so on. Pegs 1 and 11 were already being used so I used peg 6 and Fiona used the peg opposite mine. Sophia used the peg at the end of my row and Jade used the peg next to hers.

11 Which peg did Fiona use? _____
12 Which peg did Sophia use? _____
13 Which peg did Jade use? _____
14 What number was the peg opposite Sophia's? _____
15 What number was the peg opposite Jade's? _____

If f = 1, l = 2, o = 3, a = 4 and t = 5, what are the totals of these words?

16 loft _____ **17** flat _____ **18** foal _____

19 tool _____ **20** loaf _____

Underline the one word in each group that **cannot be made** from the letters of the word in capital letters.

Example	STATIONERY	stone	tyres	ration	<u>nation</u>	noisy
21	BACKING	king	gain	nick	bake	bank
22	DWINDLE	wind	lend	wide	line	dead
23	TRAINED	rind	teas	near	tide	dirt
24	PLEASING	ping	nail	pale	sign	song
25	FRAMING	gram	main	germ	firm	farm

Move one letter from the first word to the second word to make two new words.

Example	hunt	sip	<u>hut</u>	<u>snip</u>
26	bleed	nice	_____	_____
27	grows	seal	_____	_____
28	about	herd	_____	_____
29	trail	fist	_____	_____
30	snail	sows	_____	_____

Underline the pair of words most similar in meaning.

Example	come, go	<u>roams, wanders</u>	fear, fare
31	keep, hide	comfort, succour	sit, stand
32	help, hinder	chew, swallow	path, track
33	snug, cosy	naked, clothed	quite, quiet
34	hot, icy	cloudy, windy	cool, unflappable
35	here, there	soak, drench	off, on

The code for BREAKFAST is N ^ h D v / D 3 7. Encode each of these words using the same code.

36 FAKE _____

37 BEST _____

Decode these words using the same code as above.

38 N D 3 v _____

39 ^ D v h _____

40 / h D ^ _____

Give the missing two numbers and/or letters in the following sequences.

Example	2	4	6	8	10	12
41	20	25	___	35	40	___
42	___	6	9	12	___	18
43	H2	G4	F6	E8	___	___
44	1A	2Z	___	___	5W	6V
45	3m	___	5o	___	7q	8r

RUNNY   RAPID   RELAY   ROUND   RISKY

If these words are put into alphabetical order, which comes:

46 second? _____

47 fourth? _____

48 fifth? _____

A B C D E F G H I J K L M N O P Q R S T U V W X Y Z

If the days of the week are put into alphabetical order, which comes:

49 last? _____

50 after Friday? _____

Underline the word in the brackets that is most opposite in meaning to the word in capitals.

Example WIDE (broad vague long <u>narrow</u> motorway)

51 LIGHT (pale weight dark night lamp)
52 IN (fashionable clear on out around)
53 PAST (gone future history part patch)
54 LEFT (dropped missing right stay play)
55 FASTEN (attach tie bind secure untie)

Fill in the crosswords so that all the given words are included. You have been given one letter as a clue in each crossword.

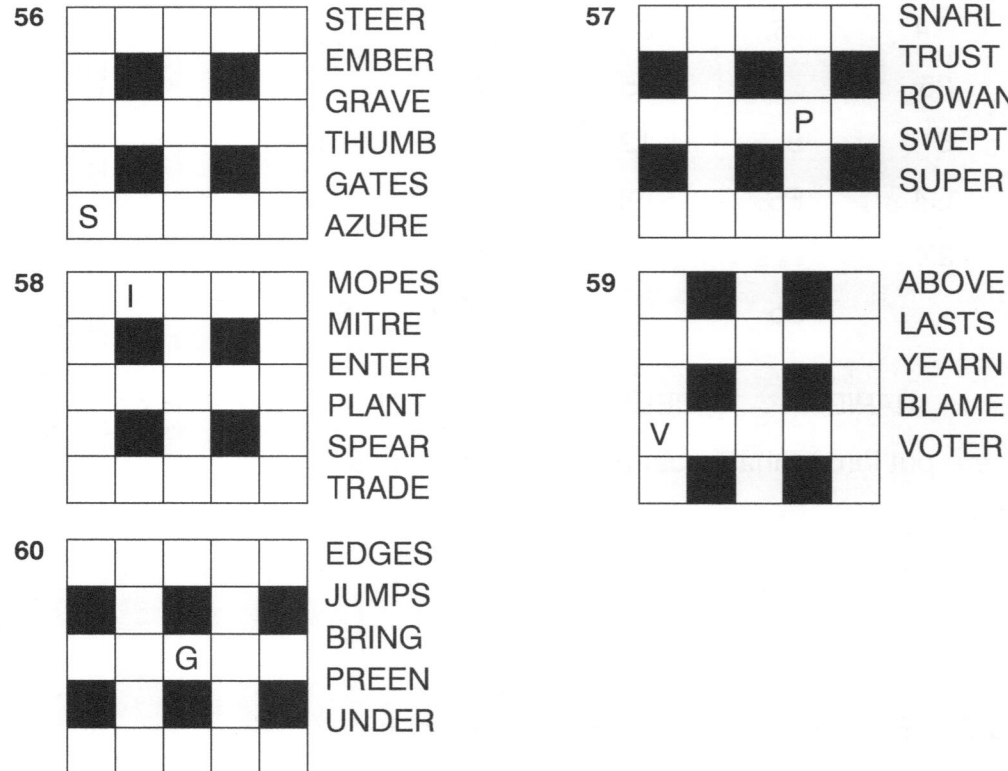

56 STEER EMBER GRAVE THUMB GATES AZURE

57 SNARL TRUST ROWAN SWEPT SUPER

58 MOPES MITRE ENTER PLANT SPEAR TRADE

59 ABOVE LASTS YEARN BLAME VOTER

60 EDGES JUMPS BRING PREEN UNDER